Debussy Claude
1850154856

972.94
(WS)

972.94

Debussy Claude
1850154856

L035901
CORNWALL SCHOOLS LIBRARY SERVICE

CORNWALL COUNTY COUNCIL
LIBRARIES AND ARTS DEPARTMENT
Education Library Services

The World's Greatest Composers

Claude Debussy

by Roderic Dunnett

OTHER TITLES IN THE SERIES
Johann Sebastian Bach by Charlotte Gray (1-85015-311-6)
Ludwig van Beethoven by Pam Brown (1-85015-302-7)
Leonard Bernstein by David Wilkins (1-85015-487-2)
Frederic Chopin by Pam Brown (1-85015-310-8)
Antonin Dvorak by Roderic Dunnett (1-85015-486-4)
Edvard Grieg by Wendy Thompson (1-85015-488-0)
Elton John by John O'Mahony (1-85015-369-8)
John Lennon by Michael White (1-85015-304-3)
Bob Marley by Marsha Bronson (1-85015-312-4)
Wolfgang Amadeus Mozart by Michael White (1-85015-300-0)
Franz Schubert by Barrie Carson Turner (1-85015-494-5)
Peter Ilyich Tchaikovsky by Michael Pollard (1-85015-303-5)
Antonio Vivaldi by Pam Brown (1-85015-301-9)

Debussy picture credits: AKG Berlin: Cover; AKG London: 8-9, 10, 16(left)/Rossetti, Dante Gabriel 1828-1882, "Prosepina", Tate Gallery, London, 16(right)/Whistler, James MacNeill, 1834-1903, "At the Piano", 18, 19/Monet, Claude 1840-1926, "Palazzo Contarini", Kunstmuseum, 20, 21, 22, 23, 25, 33/Moreau, Gustave, 1826-1898, "The Sirens", Musee Gustave Moreau, Paris, 34, 37, 39, 45, 52 (both), 59, 60; Private collection/Bridgeman Art Library: 26; Claude Debussy Museum collection, Saint-Germain-en-Laye/M.Chevalier-Joly: 4; Clive Barda/London: 58; Edimedia: 5/Bakst, Leon, 1866-1929, "Le faune", Wadsworth Atheneum, Hartford, 27, 29, 47, 50, 51; Gamma: 12 (right)/Alain le Bot, 48/Ulf Andersen; Grand Hotel, Eastbourne, The: 42-43; Image Select 6, 7 (both), 11, 12 (left), 14, 24, 30, 31, 32, 43, 44, 56; Images: 36, 40-41; Popperfoto: 35; Spectrum: 13, 54-55.

The publishers wish to extend a special thanks to the Claude Debussy Museum, Saint-Germain-en-Laye for their help on picture research.

To my father and mother.

Published in Great Britain in 1995
by Exley Publications Ltd,
16 Chalk Hill, Watford,
Herts WD1 4BN, United Kingdom.

Copyright © Exley Publications, 1995
Text copyright © Roderic Dunnett, 1995

A copy of the CIP data is available from the British Library on request.

ISBN 1-85015-485-6

All rights reserved. No part of this publication may be reproduced or transmitted in any form or by any means, electronic or mechanical, including photocopy, recording or any information storage and retrieval system without permission in writing from the Publisher.

Editor: Helen Lanz
Editorial assistant: Alison MacTier
Musical adviser: Jill Simms
Picture editors: Alex Goldberg and James Clift of Image Select
Typeset by Delta Print, Watford, Herts, U.K.
Printed at Oriental Press, – UAE.

Claude
DEBUSSY

by Roderic Dunnett

EXLEY

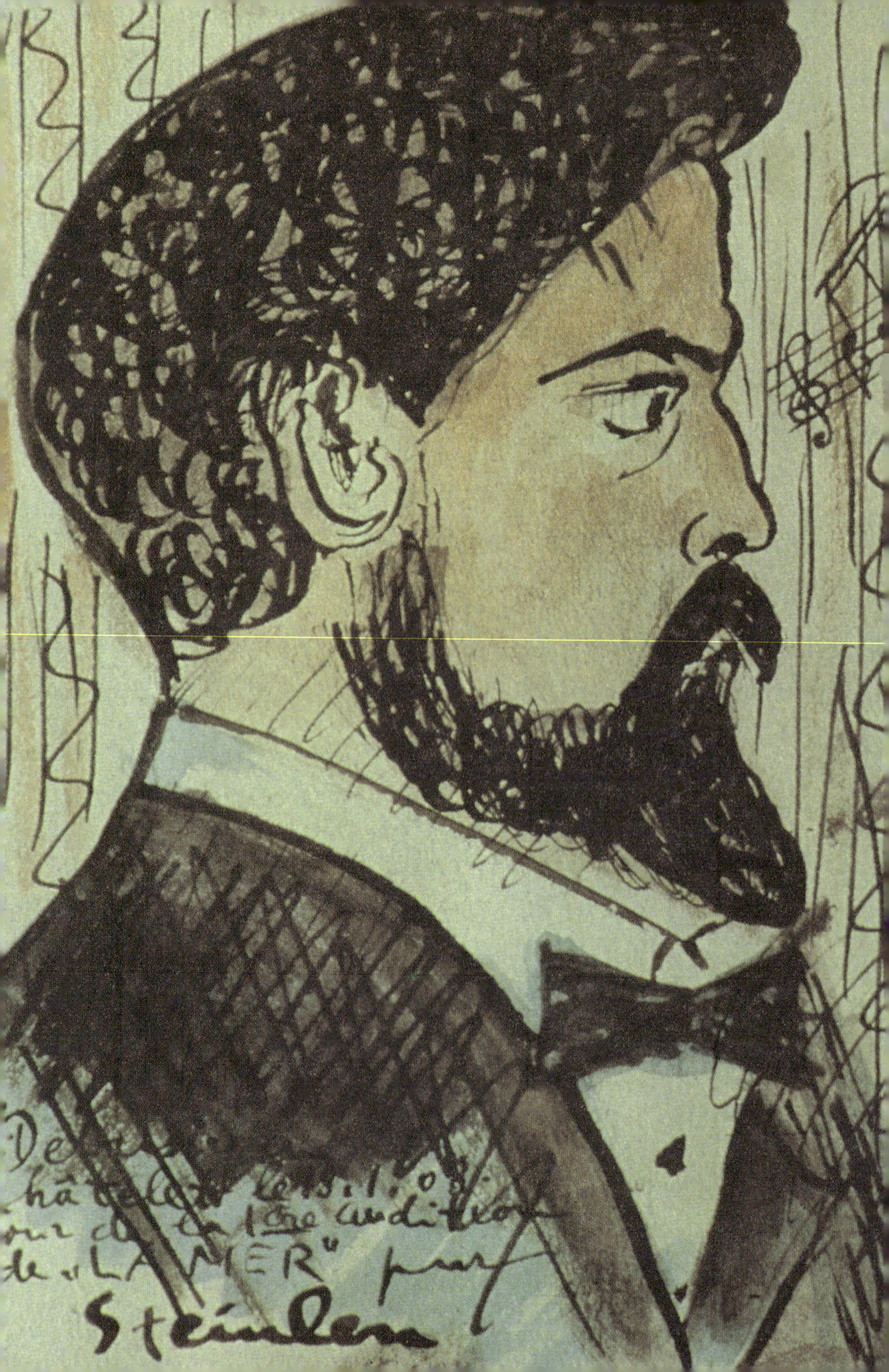
1re audition
de "LA MER" par
Steinlen

A routine concert

It was a wintry December evening in 1894. The Paris audience was gathering for a concert by the Societe Nationale at the Salle d'Harcourt. A few flicked through their copies of *Le Figaro.* Others took out a pair of lorgnettes, or glasses, and peered curiously at the musical line-up. The orchestra began tuning up. What kind of music would they hear tonight?

A violin concerto by Saint-Saens – that should be safe enough. Like many French composers, he wrote in a traditional, Romantic style. And the elderly Belgian composer, Cesar Franck, though more progressive, was well known to them from his organ recitals at the Eglise de St. Clothilde.

But Glazunov, Ropartz, Debussy – these were new, less familiar names – still young composers, scarcely over the age of thirty. Some of the titles sounded intriguing, such as: *The Wave and the Bell, The Forest,* and the *Prelude to 'The Afternoon of a Faun.'*

Creatures in the sun

A number of people in the audience may have known the poem *L'Apres-midi d'un faune* by the French poet Stephane Mallarme, on which Debussy based his famous composition.

It is a beautiful poem, although unusual, like all Mallarme's writings. Full of strange, disconnected images, it describes how a goat-man or "faun" dozes off, one hot summer afternoon long ago in some distant Mediterranean country. In his sleep, he experiences strange visions and sensations. He spots some young nymphs or girls, and tries to chase them, but they run away. Was it all just a dream?

In challenging the forms and traditions of classical music and replacing them with a new style based on revolutionary ideas, Claude Debussy (left) made a huge impact on the world of music and the stage. One of his most famous works, Prelude a 'l'Apres-midi d'un faune,' *was also made into a ballet (below).*

Debussy's earliest years were spent in his birthplace, St. Germain-en-Laye (below), on the outskirts of Paris. Debussy remained deeply attached to the city all his life, although he expressed mixed feelings about it, sometimes referring to it as a prison, sometimes as home.

Debussy's music began. First a solo flute played a sensuous chromatic pattern, where the harmony wafts up and down in semitones. It all seemed rather vague – not in any normal key at all!

Then there were harp, horns and strings, and next an oboe, until finally the whole orchestra was producing a great wash of warm, rich sound. The music's focus seemed to keep shifting – it never settled. There didn't even seem to be a real tune, or even a firm beat – just a few fragments of melody, jumbled up in strange rhythms.

Other passages sounded almost oriental. Yet none of it sounded much like any of the French music the audience knew. It was all a bit perplexing.

But it was also seductive and appealing. These voluptuous sounds, with all their great sadness and languor, made an immediate, and unusually beautiful, impression. And by the end of Debussy's ten-minute piece, many members of the audience clearly liked it. They clapped enthusiastically.

Lukewarm critics

The critics didn't enthuse much in the papers the next day, and a few people – even other composers who might have been broader-minded – were distinctly rude and scathing about it.

It was pretty, but lacked form, they said. It wasn't really music. The harmonies were unstable and unclear. It used strange scales. What was worse, *it broke all the rules.* You just weren't allowed to write music like that!

But Debussy paid no attention. He believed you could. After a great deal of pain and effort, he seemed to have found his own voice. He had composed something that finally matched the dream he had of a new, radical, and forward-looking French musical style.

Just as in art and literature a great many of the traditional forms were being challenged by "Impressionism" and "Symbolism," so Debussy introduced equally important changes in music. He enjoyed the company of writers and artists and was influenced and inspired by their radical ideas.

Debussy's music felt fresh – it was entirely original and his own. Mallarme was delighted. "Your music has breathed a true radiance into my poem," he confided to the young composer.

Even though recognition came slowly in his own country, Debussy never looked back. Today *Prelude a 'l'Apres-midi d'un faune'* is played by all the world's major orchestras. It is widely acknowledged as a masterpiece.

And with works like *La Mer, Images, Nocturnes,* and his opera *Pelleas and Melisande,* Debussy went on to establish himself as one of the world's greatest twentieth-century composers.

Above: The Debussy family's first home in Paris, No. 38 rue au Pain, is now the Maison Claude Debussy, or Debussy Museum. It contains many pictures, manuscripts, and artifacts relating to the composer's life.

Below: In his early years Achille, or "Chilo," had already begun his lifelong habit of disguising his protruding forehead with a hat, as shown in this rare early photograph.

An unusual boy

Achille-Claude Debussy was born on August 22, 1862. He was the eldest child of Manuel-Achille and Victorine Debussy. His parents ran a small china shop at thirty-eight rue au Pain, St. Germain-en-Laye, then a village just outside Paris.

After the French war with Prussia ended, civil war broke out in Paris. Debussy's father fought on the side of the Commune, which supported change against the existing government. He led one of the battles and was defeated and sentenced to four years in prison. Madame Debussy pleaded with the authorities and he was released after serving one year.

Achille (as he was called in childhood) was a curious-looking small boy. His upper head was misshapen by what was known as a "double-front," a benign bone swelling in his forehead. Later he became understandably sensitive about this, and often tried to hide it with a lock of hair brushed forward.

The Debussy family moved into Paris while Achille was still small, due to the failure of the china shop. By this time, Achille had a younger sister, Adele. Three younger brothers followed soon after.

Growing up in a large city must have been an unsettling time for the young Achille. The economic climate was at times unstable. His father found it hard to keep a steady job for long. The family moved several times, and never had much money.

"[Debussy] was uncommunicative and closed in upon himself, liking neither his lessons nor his games.... He would spend whole days sitting on a chair thinking, no one knew of what."

Debussy's sister, from The Master Musicians by Edward Lockspeiser.

Civil war

Then in 1870, when he was nearly eight, France went to war with Prussia, the leading state of Germany, and lost. German soldiers were stationed in Paris. Some even stayed in the house Achille visited for piano lessons.

War against Prussia was followed by a fierce civil war a year later, as the French could not settle on one style of government. Barricades were erected in the streets as the left-wing "Commune" fought the right-wing government. Like many poor ex-servicemen, Debussy's father joined the Commune, but he was captured in battle and remained in prison, in harsh conditions, for almost a year.

"I believe a composer must forge his own forms out of the many influences that play upon him and never close his ears to any part of the world of sound."

Henry Cowell, from The Hutchinson Encyclopedia.

Paris in the 1890s was, as now, a city of great elegance and style. Debussy, although himself from relatively humble beginnings, loved middle- or upper middle-class fashions and lifestyles, and this was reflected in his choice of friends and pursuits.

The family never recovered from the memory of this disgrace. It was a period Debussy rarely talked about in later years.

Things might have been worse, had not a kindly relative lent a hand. Achille's aunt and godmother, Clementine Roustan, took over the main responsibility for looking after the other Debussy children. For a short time, Achille alone remained with his parents.

But he also visited his aunt at Cannes, on the Mediterranean Sea. He later recalled, "I remember the railway that passed in front of the house and the sea that stretched as far as the horizon. Sometimes you could imagine that the railway came right out of the sea or went into it."

Such memories stayed with him. Many years later he would entitle one of his most famous works *La Mer – The Sea.*

Toward the Conservatoire

It was Clementine who first encouraged Achille's musical gifts, by arranging for him to have piano lessons with a young local teacher.

When Achille returned to Paris, he began to have lessons with a new teacher, Madame Maute de Fleurville, a distinguished woman who had known many famous people, including, it was claimed, even the Polish composer Frederic Chopin. She was a fine and perceptive teacher, and she soon became convinced of Achille's talent. The very next year she entered him for the famous Paris Conservatoire.

Entry to the Conservatoire was by examination and a scholarship paid for by the state. There were thirty-eight candidates of all ages. To the surprise and delight of his parents, Achille, who was one of the youngest, was included among only eight successful award-winners.

So in October 1872, Achille Debussy, aged just ten, embarked on one of the most formative periods of his life. A great new journey of musical discovery had begun for him.

Although he won several prizes, Debussy's years at the Conservatoire were by no means easy or trouble-free. The impression that the square-headed boy in the sailor suit made on both teachers and fellow students was mixed.

Initially he seemed rather surly. He tended to rush at the piano, breathing heavily and playing unnecessarily forcefully. While he was seen as a pianist of promise, he was not at all the natural virtuoso his parents had hoped.

Steady progress

Nonetheless, he made steady progress as a pupil in the piano class. "The piano doesn't excite him," commented his shrewd teacher, the elderly Antoine Marmontel, "but music certainly does!" (In fact, much of Debussy's finest music would later be written for the piano.)

But it was in Albert Lavignac's *solfege* group that Achille made quickest progress. *Solfege* was a new system, designed to teach basic harmony and to lay the foundations for composition. It suited Achille's talents well. From the ages of eleven to thirteen, he won an annual summer prize for *solfege*.

Lavignac, who had only recently arrived, was one of the younger teachers at the Conservatoire. He took an increasing interest in his rather intense pupil. One winter evening, the two stayed on late together and played through a four-hand version of Richard Wagner's opera *Tannhauser*, which had just caused a stir at the Paris Opera. The two became so absorbed in its novel harmonies and sound qualities that they were locked in! They had to find their way down to the street in the dark.

Wagner was thought to be the most revolutionary composer of the middle and late nineteenth century. His music was to have a profound influence on the young French student.

The rebel

At the age of fifteen Achille was no longer winning any prizes. Nor was he successful the following year. His parents lost all hope of their son ever becoming the rich and famous pianist they had dreamed of.

The Paris Conservatoire was the leading school of music in France throughout the nineteenth and much of the twentieth centuries. By Debussy's time, however, many of the music schools of Europe had become fixed in their ways, rooted in the Classic-Romantic tradition. His rebellious attitude was mainly against this refusal to change.

"Debussy would make an excellent pupil if he were less sketchy and cavalier."
Emile Durand, 1878.

Right: Tuning a piano regularly is essential in order to keep it in prime working order and ensure the instrument's "harmonics" sound correctly. Debussy often worked at the keyboard while composing.

Above: By the time Claude Debussy was eighteen, he had already won numerous prizes for his musical abilities. He was now also about to embark on his first serious attempts at composing.

There were other causes for concern. Achille had turned into a rebellious teenage pupil. He disagreed openly with his teachers, and he was more than once nearly expelled.

Many of the Conservatoire's staff believed that the musical rules and principles that were a century or more old should not be changed. Achille openly disagreed. Though he made progress in some of his studies, he soon came to despise the old-fashioned assumptions that prevailed in the musty, crumbling old building on the corner of the rue Bergere.

Then in 1880, at the age of eighteen, a first prize in his practical harmony group enabled him, at last, to progress to a composition class.

A new friend

His new composition teacher, Ernest Guiraud, was impressed by Debussy. He listened carefully to his young pupil's new-fangled theories and was prepared to take him seriously. They argued and debated together incessantly, both in and out of class.

Guiraud's teaching studio was close to the Debussy family's top-floor apartment in the rue Pigalle. Teacher and pupil would often meet in the cafes to chat or play billiards together in the evening. Guiraud's advice proved a very important formative influence – as well as a wise, restraining one – on his headstrong young pupil.

Debussy's journey

There were other new openings. In 1880 a wealthy Russian widow, Madame Nadezhda von Meck, who was also the patroness of the Russian composer Tchaikovsky, wrote to request a pianist to tutor and accompany the younger members of her family. The tutor was also required to accompany her in sight-reading keyboard duets, and to play the piano part in her private piano trio.

Whatever reservations he may have once had, Debussy's former teacher (who once described his playing as "irresponsible and muddle-headed") recommended the young Achille.

That summer he spent four months with Madame von Meck and her large family, staying in fine mansions in Switzerland, France, and Italy. They visited Rome and Florence, and the next year he also stayed with them in Russia.

This was the first real insight Achille got into the wider world beyond Paris. During these idyllic summers he became almost a member of the von Meck family. When he was not teaching the children, he played games with them and they gave each other nicknames. "He enlivens the whole house, and is a marvellous mimic," wrote Madame von Meck. "He is so good-humoured, also satisfied with everything and entertains our people tremendously." He even proposed marriage, in jest, to thirteen year old Sophie.

The great domed Renaissance cathedral of Florence, the European city of art and architecture, has always attracted many foreign visitors. Debussy visited the city on his travels with the von Meck family.

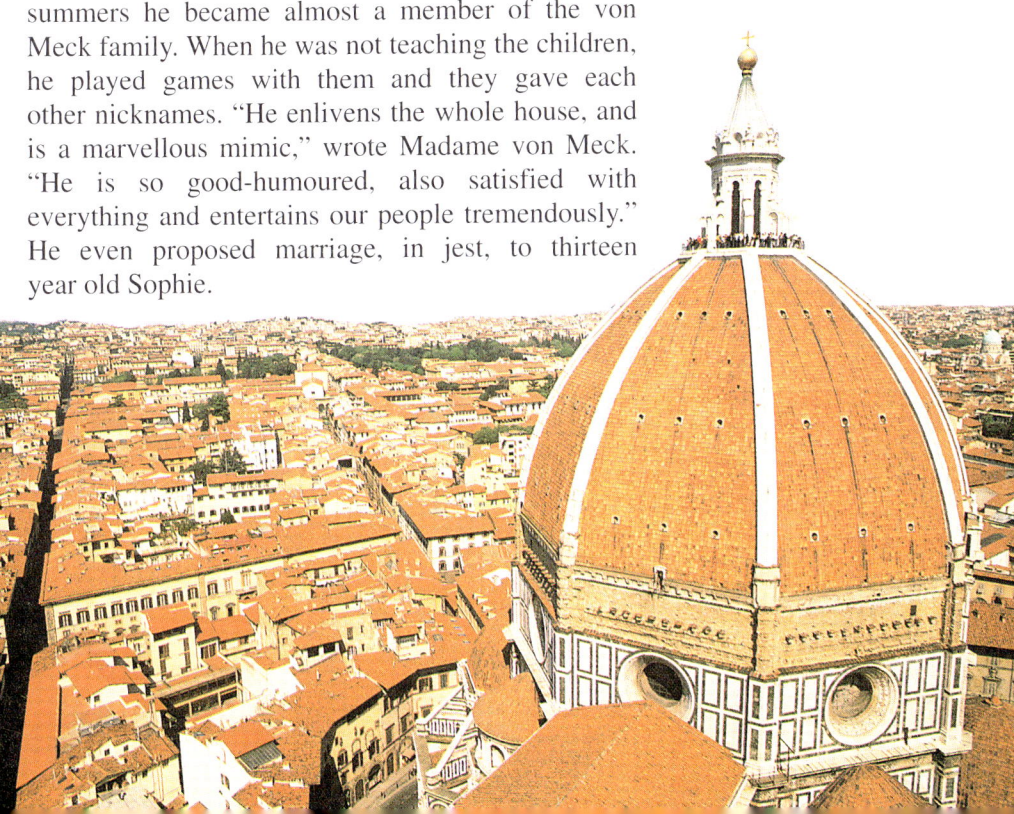

The young Debussy often became deeply attached to people who treated him as one of their own family. It was perhaps a sign of his deep insecurity – an inner loneliness – which never really left him.

The composer emerges

By now Achille was writing music. He composed some songs and a piano trio in Florence, and later he sent Madame von Meck a short Symphony in B minor for piano with four hands. It is an early work, and shows little of his later originality.

Once back in Paris, in 1881, Debussy became the organist for a famous choral society, in order to make a little money. He was also engaged as a pianist to accompany pupils of the singing teacher, Madame Moreau-Sainti.

One of these pupils, Madame Marie-Blanche Vasnier, was married to a well-to-do civil servant. The young student visited the Vasniers at their home, and was soon allowed daily use of the piano at their house in the rue de Constantinople. This became virtually a "second home" for him.

The Vasnier house must have seemed very different from the Debussys' cramped apartment. In the drawing room he would walk ceaselessly up and down, rolling his cigarettes while humming or composing in his head, then return to the piano to write the music down.

He also visited the family at their house outside Paris. There, he would play through his songs with Madame Vasnier, or they would go for walks, play croquet, and engage in animated conversation, before he reluctantly caught the last train home.

Often he borrowed books from Monsieur Vasnier, extending his knowledge of English literature and of the French poets, whose work he was already starting to set to music.

First love

Though Achille's friendship with both Vasniers was close, the intense young student soon fell deeply in love with Madame Vasnier, who was a few years

Claude Debussy spent long hours at the Vasniers' house, where he was encouraged to read and discuss works of literature. Madame Marie-Blanche Vasnier, a society lady some four years older than the young musician, became the focus of his love and the inspiration for several of his early compositions.

his senior. "I know this passion is mad," he wrote later to a close friend, "but that's what prevents me from being logical. My feelings have only become more acute. I feel I have not sacrificed enough to my love of her."

For a time, Madame Vasnier became Debussy's "muse," or artistic inspiration – the thought of her alone inspired him to compose. More than twenty of his youthful songs were dedicated to her. Not surprisingly, their close relationship attracted a certain amount of Parisian gossip.

> *"He used to compose at the piano...or at times walking about the room.... When he had found what he wanted, he began to write. He made few corrections, but he spent a long time working things out in his head and at the piano before he wrote."*
> Madame Vasnier's daughter.

A reluctant winner

As the time neared for his graduation from the Conservatoire, Debussy was encouraged to aim for the highest prize of all – the prestigious Prix de Rome, awarded by the Academie des Beaux Arts to outstanding painters, sculptors, and musicians. This prize gave the winner three years' private study at the Villa Medici, an impressive hill-top mansion in Rome.

Debussy's previous attempt at the competition, a cantata entitled *Le Gladiateur,* achieved only second prize. This time he heard that his new cantata, *L'Enfant prodigue – The Prodigal Son,* a rather conventional work written in a rapid three weeks under exam conditions, had won him the 1884 Prix de Rome.

His reaction was typical in its awkwardness. "I was standing on the Pont des Arts," he later recalled, "watching the boats on the River Seine, and the sunlight playing on the water. Someone suddenly ran up, tapped me on the shoulder and said, 'You've won first prize!' Suddenly all my pleasure vanished. I felt I was no longer free."

So, in January 1885, Achille-Claude Debussy set off for Rome at the age of twenty-two.

Prisoner in Rome

The Villa Medici, a large house set amid gardens on a hillside in Rome's city suburbs, seemed to him cold and unwelcoming. He had to share a room with five others, and complained of biting insects in summer and the biting cold in winter. He saw the building as

The paintings of Dante Gabriel Rossetti, a founder of the English pre-Raphaelite school of painting (above), and James McNeill Whistler, the British Impressionist painter (above right), both inspired Debussy.

a prison, and found the conversation of his former musician friends tiresome and their attitudes to music too traditional. They were not natural rebels as he was.

He got along better with his fellow art students. Together they enthused about painters, such as Dante Gabriel Rossetti and James McNeill Whistler. Each of these artists was to be an important influence on Debussy's own future artistic development.

Debussy was still seeking a musical voice of his own, free of the stifling nineteenth-century French and German traditions, which were so bound up with sonatas and symphonies, and stale fixed "rules" of harmony laid down many years earlier by others.

"A dissonant chord would almost cause a revolution," he declared scornfully after a visit to the opera. "As there are no precedents, I must create new forms," he wrote to his old friend, Monsieur Vasnier.

Early influences

The music of the German composer Richard Wagner, broke all the boundaries of earlier opera. It was filled with lush chromatic harmonies, use of recurring musical phrases, and new methods of relating words to music. For these reasons, it was of particular interest to the young, radical Debussy.

Debussy already had a score of Wagner's opera *Tristan and Isolde*, which was full of strange, beguiling harmonies. This mythical tale of two lovers who are united in death captivated him. He explored it and analyzed it, playing it through many times, alone or with others at the Villa Medici.

Tristan would re-emerge, completely transformed, in Debussy's own *Prelude a 'l'Apres-midi d'un faune.'* Later on, he even planned a Tristan opera of his own.

Finding his own voice

Each student at the Villa Medici was expected to send home a series of works, known as *envois*, submitted for the judgment of the Academie in Paris.

Debussy's first *envoi*, completed in 1886, was *Zuleima*, a cantata based on words by the popular German poet, Heinrich Heine, who also wrote these words: "The mysterious island of the spirits was vaguely outlined by shafts of moonlight; delicious sounds emanated from it; nebulous dances floated over it. The sounds became gradually sweeter and the dances whirled on more excitedly.... Meanwhile we two hopelessly drifted over the vast sea." Few quotes capture more successfully the themes that obsessed Debussy for much of his life – mystery, the sea, islands, elusive half-heard sounds, floating dances, and situations that seem hopelessly out of control.

Debussy was very much ahead of his time. Despite its rather traditional theme of forbidden romance between a Moor and a Christian, the conservative Paris judges' panel found *Zuleima* "incomprehensible" and "bizarre".

Another piece that Debussy worked on in Rome was *Diane au bois – Diana in the Forest* – an attractive story of the goddess Diana and her conquest by Eros, or Love. It was based on a work by Theodore de Banville, Debussy's most loved poet at the time. Debussy never finished it, but from what he did complete, there are clear signs that it played a very important role in his emergence as a fresh, innovative, and original composer.

"Composers aren't daring enough. Music is freer than perhaps any other art-form, since it doesn't have to try to reproduce nature exactly, but is able to explore the mysterious relationship between nature and imagination."
Claude Debussy.

Above: Franz Liszt helped pave the way for Debussy through piano works that influenced the music of Richard Wagner and opened the door to the fresh new musical thinking of the early twentieth century.

Right: Debussy was a great lover and collector of art, and many of his friends were artists. In one sense he regarded his work in the same way as an Impressionist painting – the composer was a craftsman who worked with sound and silence in the way that artists worked with light and shadow.

Liszt and Palestrina

Despite his reservations about his time in Rome, it did provide Debussy with the opportunity to meet the great composer-pianist Franz Liszt in 1885. He heard the remarkable quality of Liszt's piano playing, especially his subtle use of the pedals, which seemed to make the music "breathe."

This had an important influence on the piano works of Debussy. He himself had a remarkable touch on the piano. The very old recordings that still exist of him playing his own pieces are models of clarity.

While in Rome, Debussy was increasingly attracted to the choral music by the great Renaissance composers such as Palestrina and Lassus. Their mastery of counterpoint, the musical technique of combining melodies, and skilled use of plainsong, or medieval chant, made a deep impression on him.

Back home

By the end of his second year in Rome, Debussy had had enough. "I'd rather do twice as much work in Paris than drag out this life here," he wrote to Monsieur Vasnier. He clearly felt lonely and Rome, despite all its fine art treasures, bored him.

He was short of money, almost three-quarters of his scholarship had to be paid out in board and lodgings, and unlike some of the other students, he did not have a rich family able to support him with cash for extra comforts.

As soon as his required two years' study were up in 1887, he set off for home, taking with him the draft of a new work, *Printemps – Spring*. This was inspired by the famous Renaissance painting *La Primavera* by Botticelli, and by other works of art.

In *Printemps* Debussy uses orchestra and a female chorus to suggest, as he puts it, "the slow and miserable birth of beings and things in nature, their gradual blossoming, and finally the joy of being born into some new life."

The sensual opening using flute, oboe, and harp, with its hints of the whole-tone scale, gives an early taste of his *Prelude a 'l'Apres-midi d'un faune,'* while the wordless choruses anticipate the later *Nocturnes*.

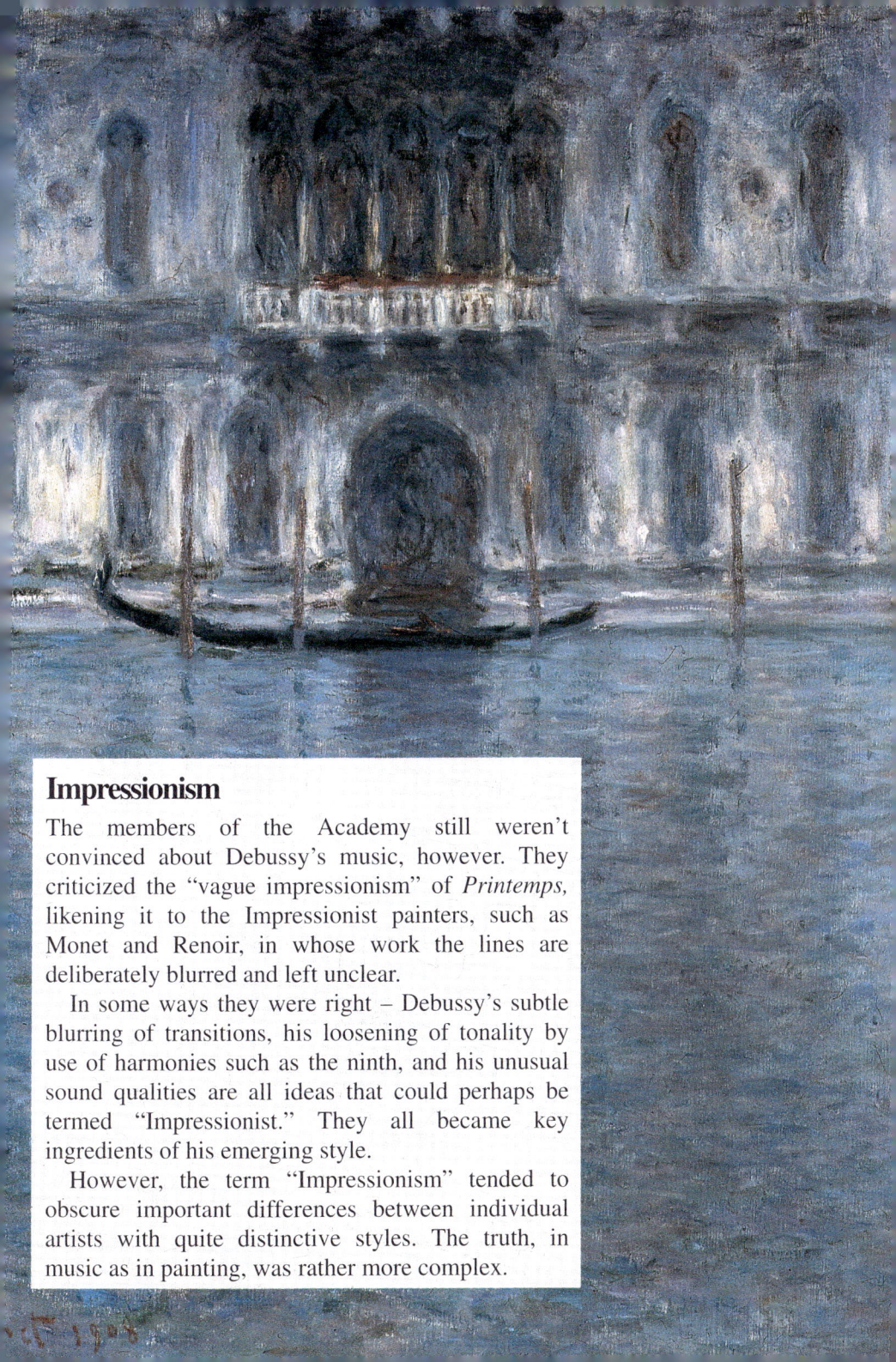

Impressionism

The members of the Academy still weren't convinced about Debussy's music, however. They criticized the "vague impressionism" of *Printemps*, likening it to the Impressionist painters, such as Monet and Renoir, in whose work the lines are deliberately blurred and left unclear.

In some ways they were right – Debussy's subtle blurring of transitions, his loosening of tonality by use of harmonies such as the ninth, and his unusual sound qualities are all ideas that could perhaps be termed "Impressionist." They all became key ingredients of his emerging style.

However, the term "Impressionism" tended to obscure important differences between individual artists with quite distinctive styles. The truth, in music as in painting, was rather more complex.

La vie Parisienne

On his return to Paris, Debussy tried to begin composing again. Initially he lived at home, cushioned by his final year's grant from the Academy.

But only a month after his return, his father, now aged fifty, was dismissed from his job as a bookkeeper at the Compagnie des Fives-Lille. It looked as if Debussy might be needed as a breadwinner.

But these difficulties appear to have been overcome, for the family soon moved to a larger apartment over a courtyard on the fourth floor in the rue de Berlin. This gave Debussy, now approaching twenty-five, a little independence. He even had his own private entrance.

He soon began visiting bars once more and enjoying the cafe life of Paris, a city full of sparkle during the lively years at the close of the nineteenth century. Often he relied on others – musical or literary friends – to help him out in those times by giving or lending him money.

The cafes of Paris were regular haunts for Debussy in the early years following his return from Rome. Here he would meet with literary and musical friends to play billiards, discuss issues about which they felt strongly, or simply pass the time of day.

"La Damoiselle elue"

In Paris, Debussy quickly became friends with other talented composers, such as Paul Dukas and Ernest Chausson. They helped promote a performance of his next important work, *La Damoiselle elue – The Blessed Damozel*.

Painters of the English pre-Raphaelite movement, such as Dante Gabriel Rossetti and Edward Burne-Jones, with their depiction of heroic and chivalrous themes, were almost as much in fashion in Paris at this time as Wagner's operas.

Debussy's new work was a setting of Rossetti's rather lush and dreamy text *The Blessed Damozel*, which describes how a maiden with lilies in her hair sits waiting for her heavenly lover. One critic actually likened it to the musical equivalent of a stained glass window. *La Damoiselle elue*, with its implications of an idealized love realized only in death, is a work for soloist, female chorus, and orchestra. Debussy's setting has strong echoes of Wagner. The tender soprano solo represents the image of a perfect woman, or eternal womanhood, which Debussy was to idolize, yet also betray, in his own later life.

Popular pieces

As well as some songs inspired by the French poet and critic Charles Baudelaire, which are similarly inspired by Wagner, Debussy also produced several charming, simpler works at this time – the *Petite Suite* for piano with four hands, and the two piano *Arabesques*. All of these works, thanks to the generosity of friends, soon found publishers. One of them, Jacques Durand, would later publish many of Debussy's most revolutionary pieces.

His *Suite bergamasque*, which includes the beautiful, ever-popular "Clair de lune" – "Moonlight" – reflects his fondness for the poetry of another French poet, Paul Verlaine, whom he had met at Madame Maute's. It also reflects his interest for the lively street shows of the Italian *commedia dell'arte*, or street comedy, famous for its semi-serious, semi-clownlike characters, Harlequin and Pulcinella.

Debussy, like many of his generation in the days when the hazards of smoking weren't fully understood, smoked heavily. His upright piano was covered in burn marks, showing where he had carelessly rested a cigarette or let it burn right down.

Wagner's heroic operas, or "music dramas," had a very great influence on Debussy, even though he struggled hard against being a mere imitator. Parsifal, *shown below, was in many ways the direct forerunner of Debussy's* Pelleas et Melisande.

The songs

A few of the songs Debussy composed for Madame Vasnier, such as *Beau Soir* – "Beautiful Evening" – and *Mandoline,* were published soon after his return from Rome. He had thirteen of them specially bound in a collection for her personal use. Others, such as *Les Roses,* with its excitable piano accompaniment, or the high-soaring *Le Lilas – The Lilacs –* remained unpublished until much later.

The dreamlike words of these songs give a clue to Debussy's own sensual awakening. "A Chinese girl is sleeping, swathed in crepe up to her neck, on the lake fringed by azaleas, water lilies, and bamboo. Like a pair of flowers let us join our loving lips, and wear death out with a kiss."

The Bayreuth festival

Thanks to the generosity of a friend, Debussy made two journeys to hear Wagner's operas at the great Festspielhaus in the German town of Bayreuth, firstly in 1888.

On his second visit, the following year, he heard *Tristan and Isolde,* which had so fascinated him in Rome, though by now he was beginning to grow out of its sensual harmonies. But on these journeys he was also influenced by another major work – Wagner's last opera, *Parsifal,* based on the Christian story in medieval legend of the Holy Grail, the cup used by Jesus at the Last Supper.

Parsifal's serene, brooding atmosphere was to infuse almost all Debussy's completed stage works, as well as several that he never finished.

Fascinating new sounds

While Debussy was away in Germany, in 1889, a grand new metal construction had begun to loom over the Champ de Mars in Paris. The famous Eiffel Tower, originally planned as a temporary display, still dominates the city's skyline today.

Paris staged the "Exposition Universelle," a huge international exhibition, later that year. At this event, countless nations of the world showed off their products, together with attractive, lively displays of national art, music, folklore, and dance.

What especially caught Debussy's imagination were some strange musical instruments from the East – the "gamelan," orchestras of Java and Indonesia, with their muffled sound of gongs played with bamboo, and the curious flutes and strange, weird scales and harmonies of the music that accompanied the drama performers of Annam (present-day Cambodia and Vietnam).

There were also concerts of Russian music, at which Debussy heard for the first time an attractive but austere orchestral piece called *Night on Bald Mountain,* by a highly individual Russian composer, Modeste Mussorgsky, whose works were to influence him increasingly over the next few years.

Toward an opera

With many musical themes and styles in his head, Debussy was also seeking a text for an opera. First of all he embarked on a collaboration with the poet

The Exposition Universelle, held beneath the huge new Eiffel Tower in Paris, caused great excitement in the capital and attracted visitors from around the world. It was here that Debussy and his friends first heard gypsy music from Hungary and folk music from Europe, Africa, and the East. These new sounds became influential to the young composer's music.

Arnold Schoenberg, like Claude Debussy, was seeking a way forward from the sentimentalism of the late Romantic composers. Debussy placed an emphasis on varying patterns rather than symphonic developments in music. Schoenberg likewise developed his own new forms of musical improvisation.

Catulle Mendes, a larger-than-life literary figure who shared his love of Wagner.

Debussy worked on *Rodrigue et Chimene* for almost two years. It was a love story about the famous Spanish champion against the Moors, Rodrigo of Bivar, who was known as "El Cid." Yet with two acts completed, filling more than 120 pages, Debussy sent the text back to Mendes and abandoned the project. He felt that the spirit of Richard Wagner was too strong to shake off. His own style was being stifled.

Debussy never did wholly shake off the influence of Wagner. Rather, it was he, together with other composers, such as Arnold Schoenberg and Gustav Mahler, who did the most to develop Wagner's musical ideas a logical stage further, and to adapt them for the twentieth century.

What Debussy was really seeking was something entirely new, an operatic idiom of his own. "I need," he said, "a text by a poet who, resorting to discreet suggestion … will enable me to graft my dream upon his dream." The works of Theodore de Banville and the American poet Edgar Allan Poe both seemed to offer possibilities. But the man who most helped Debussy to create an opera that would stand as one of the great achievements of twentieth century was the Belgian poet and dramatist Maurice Maeterlinck.

Maeterlinck and Symbolism

Maeterlinck was a Belgian poet whose style seemed quite unlike anyone else's. In 1893 Debussy saw a brand new play by Maeterlinck. It was called *Pelleas et Melisande*. He bought a copy of the play from a bookstall on a Paris street and read it eagerly. It was to change his whole life.

The sense of mystery in *Pelleas et Melisande* is very strong. Things are only half-expressed – place, character, and action are suggested with the lightest of touches, so subtly that the reader or viewer has to make of it what he or she will.

The name given to poetry of this kind – suggestive rather than concrete, and shrouded in uncertainty, with the precise meaning blurred – was "Symbolism."

The early twentieth century was a period of experimentation and discovery in the arts. The painter Pablo Picasso experimented with many kinds of abstract art. Although Picasso is now regarded as the father of modern art, his work, like Debussy's, was at first seen by many as being ugly and shocking, and was met with much disapproval.

"Symbolism" was used by several important poets, such as Verlaine, Mallarme, and T. S. Eliot. The term can also be applied to novelists such as Andre Gide and Alain-Fournier or to the strange, surreal paintings of Magritte, Chagall, and Picasso.

Some might call Debussy an "Impressionist," but it was "Symbolism" that now claimed his allegiance. This was the subtle style he had been reaching out for in all his works so far – the strange, elusive worlds of *Diane au bois* and *La Damoiselle elue*, and the huge empty castle of Bivar in *Rodrigue et Chimene*. Symbolism was Debussy's destiny.

In love again

By 1893 Debussy seemed to be enjoying life. He was photographed boating on the River Marne, and playing the piano to entertain close friends at the house of his friend, the composer Ernest Chausson. He was growing in confidence.

Part of the reason was simple. He was, if not entirely happy, at least more content. He had settled

"[Pelleas et Melisande is] a work of art original in its impression, and subtle in expression.... One is overcome by the haunting sorcery and the subtle intoxication of this music."
Andre Corneau,
from Le Matin, 1902.

into a relationship with a girl from Normandy called Gabrielle Dupont. He called her Gaby, she dubbed him Claude – and Claude he remained.

Despite a few arguments and interruptions, Claude and Gaby remained together for some eight years. He moved out of his parents' home and the couple rented a small, cheap, and very plain attic apartment together in the rue de Londres in Paris.

Gabrielle, like Madame Vasnier before her, became Debussy's inspiration. He dedicated his score of *Rodrigue et Chimene* to her, and much later, even after they had broken up, he sent her an inscribed copy of *Pelleas et Melisande*, recognizing that his new opera belonged to the time he spent with her.

The two were close companions and lovers. And though Gaby was sometimes discreetly absent from Society gatherings that chose to frown on unmarried couples, the pair was often seen together in the lively smoke-filled bars and cafes of Montmartre, such as Le Chat noir or L'Auberge du clou, where Claude had met his lifelong friend, the composer Erik Satie, two years earlier.

Debussy and his girlfriend, Gabrielle Dupont, frequently visited the grand-style bars such as Chez Weber and Le Chat noir (above), as well as the smaller piano bars in Montmartre, on the hill above Paris.

Concerts

Debussy's music, which he worked on in between hours of reading, spending time with Gaby, socializing in cafes, arguing with poets and writers, and eating (he was a talented cook who loved refined, carefully prepared food), was now beginning to be heard.

Just after Christmas, a quartet led by the famous Belgian violinist Eugene Ysaye gave the first performance of his String Quartet. The flowing sounds and unusual scales of the gamelan orchestra's he had heard at the Exposition had obviously made their mark. One famous critic later recalled the work's "exquisite perfume of the Far East."

All the same, several leading quartets refused to play the composition, claiming it was "too difficult."

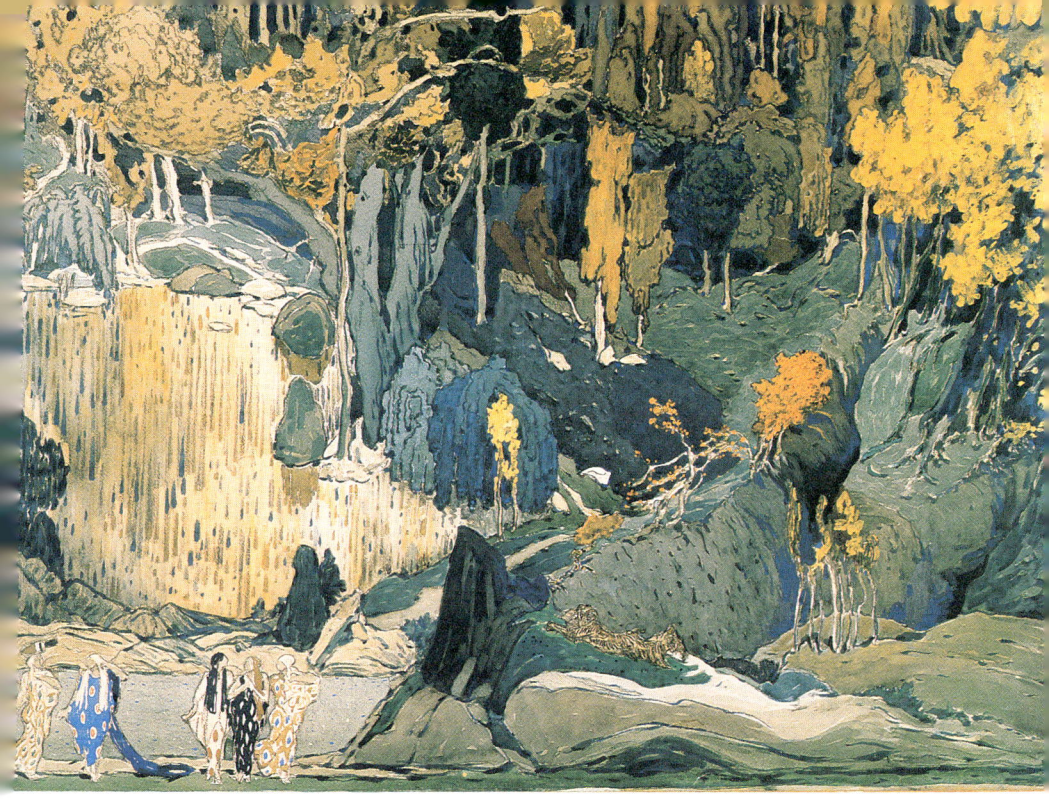

"Prelude a 'l'Apres-midi d'un faune'"

A year later, just before Christmas, on December 22, 1894, Debussy experienced his greatest triumph so far. Despite the sneerings of some critics, the audience's response that evening to *Prelude a 'l'Apres-midi d'un faune'* was so warm and enthusiastic that the young conductor, Gustave Doret, broke the normal rules and repeated the performance.

It was this musical portrayal of Stephane Mallarme's sensual poem that at last ensured Debussy's real breakthrough.

One of Debussy's most famous works, Prelude a 'l'Apres-midi d'un faune,' *received mixed reviews after its opening performance. One critic said it was one of the greatest achievements in French musical history, while another claimed that the composer had destroyed rhythm and melody in music.*

A new style

Musically, Claude had moved onto new ground. The form of the *Prelude* was wholly new and original. Traditional tonality and harmony were more flexible in Debussy's hands, and the modulations, or movement's between keys, were sudden, abrupt, and completely unexpected.

Debussy's melodies no longer followed the usual diatonic major-minor pattern, but made use of less familiar, "modal" patterns, and employed Oriental and even whole-tone scales, and chromaticism.

The rhythms became fluid, and Debussy used the orchestral tones of various instruments, such as flute, oboe, and harp, brilliantly – almost as ends in themselves. Even the silences in the piece seemed to be bursting with music. "It was hearing this work," said the young composer Maurice Ravel, "that I first understood what real music was."

The influence of Mallarme

Debussy knew Stephane Mallarme well, for he had attended many of the Tuesday evening literary sessions at the poet's house, which were known as "les mardis de la rue de Rome."

Many writers and artists from various disciplines gathered there to listen to Mallarme, who was an inspiring teacher, expounding his views on poetry and a new literary style.

It was from Mallarme and his circle, as well as from fellow composers like his friend Erik Satie, that Debussy gained the confidence to "break the rules" openly, and overturn long-regarded traditions that he scorned once and for all.

It was his natural inclination anyway – Debussy was a born radical. But the example of these people encouraged him not to turn back, or be cowardly, but determinedly to follow his own will.

The Therese debacle

In the February of 1894, urged by his friends and perhaps hankering after respectability, Claude began an engagement to a young singer, Therese Roger. Therese had sung beautifully in *La Damoiselle elue* and also gave the first performance of his *Proses lyriques,* a collection of four songs Debussy composed to rather unusual modern texts that he had written himself. Full of gentle nostalgia, they are among his best middle-period songs.

Claude and Therese saw a great deal of each other.

"If modern music may be said to have had a definite beginning, it started with the flute melody opening the Prelude a 'l'Apres-midi d'un faune' *by de Debussy."*

's, from Modern Music.

In due course, however, Claude abruptly broke off his engagement to Therese. Some of his friends felt he had behaved very badly. It was a taste of worse to come.

"Pelleas et Melisande"

Debussy had been working on his opera, *Pelleas et Melisande* for some time. He completed the first version by 1895.

Set in the mysterious, imaginary medieval kingdom of Allemonde, Maurice Maeterlinck's story tells of how a young girl, Melisande, lost in a dark forest, is found by a prince, Golaud, who takes her home to his castle. They marry and have a child. But her husband is gloomy, and his home even gloomier. Married life quickly turns into lonely trial.

Soon, Melisande falls for Golaud's younger half-brother, Pelleas. Their love is just blossoming when her husband's terrible jealousy boils over. He strikes and kills Pelleas. But he cannot regain either his wife or their former life together. Melisande dies in

In his Prelude a 'l'Apres-midi d'un faune,' *Debussy aimed to combine the exotic and the pleasurable and to produce a sound that encouraged the listener to feel rather than to think. He soon immersed himself deeply in his new opera, producing music of outstanding beauty even in the interludes that he had to compose in a last-minute panic.*

Above: The parting of Pelleas and Melisande, watched by a jealous husband, Golaud, who is poised to kill his half-brother and rival, Pelleas.

Opposite: The young Scottish soprano Mary Garden charmed Debussy with her gentle voice and was ideally suited to the shy role of Melisande. She was already popular with French audiences, having won their approval in previous operatic performances.

childbirth. Golaud is left, distraught, with the baby daughter. But whose child is it? Pelleas's or his own? He will never know.

Debussy's *Pelleas et Melisande*, with its flowing interludes, haunting melodies, and simply delivered lines, weaves a magic spell. It is an opera full of shadowy, eerie castles, strange lakes and forests. Its characters seem driven by some powerful fate or destiny. The tender scene where Melisande lets down her fair hair to Pelleas from a window is one of the most famous in all opera. *Pelleas et Melisande* remains to this day the high point of Debussy's operatic achievement.

Furthermore, it has no arias, duets, or ensembles such as appear in Italian opera, or even occasionally in Wagner, but is instead full of simply declaimed lines, which seem to echo normal speech.

Domestic upheaval

However, it was to take seven more years before Debussy's opera finally reached performance on the stage. Meanwhile, the next few years, the late eighteen-nineties, were less productive, as the composer struggled to find a way forward after *Pelleas*. He even tried his hand at writing plays.

As the new century approached, Debussy experienced some turmoil in his personal life. Several old friends died, including his publisher, Georges Hartmann, who had supported him with a regular monthly payment or "retainer" of five hundred francs. This left Claude's finances precarious.

His relationship with Gaby was under strain too. First she lost her father. Then she found a letter and learned of a secret liaison between Claude and another woman – and it was by no means Claude's first.

Not surprisingly, Gaby, fearing she might lose him, felt acutely insecure. A revolver was produced and she threatened to shoot herself, or Claude, or both – the story is not entirely clear.

Things were patched up, but not for long. In 1897, Gaby, by now aged thirty-one, left Claude for a more upper-class lover. The next year she left Paris for Normandy, where she lived until her death.

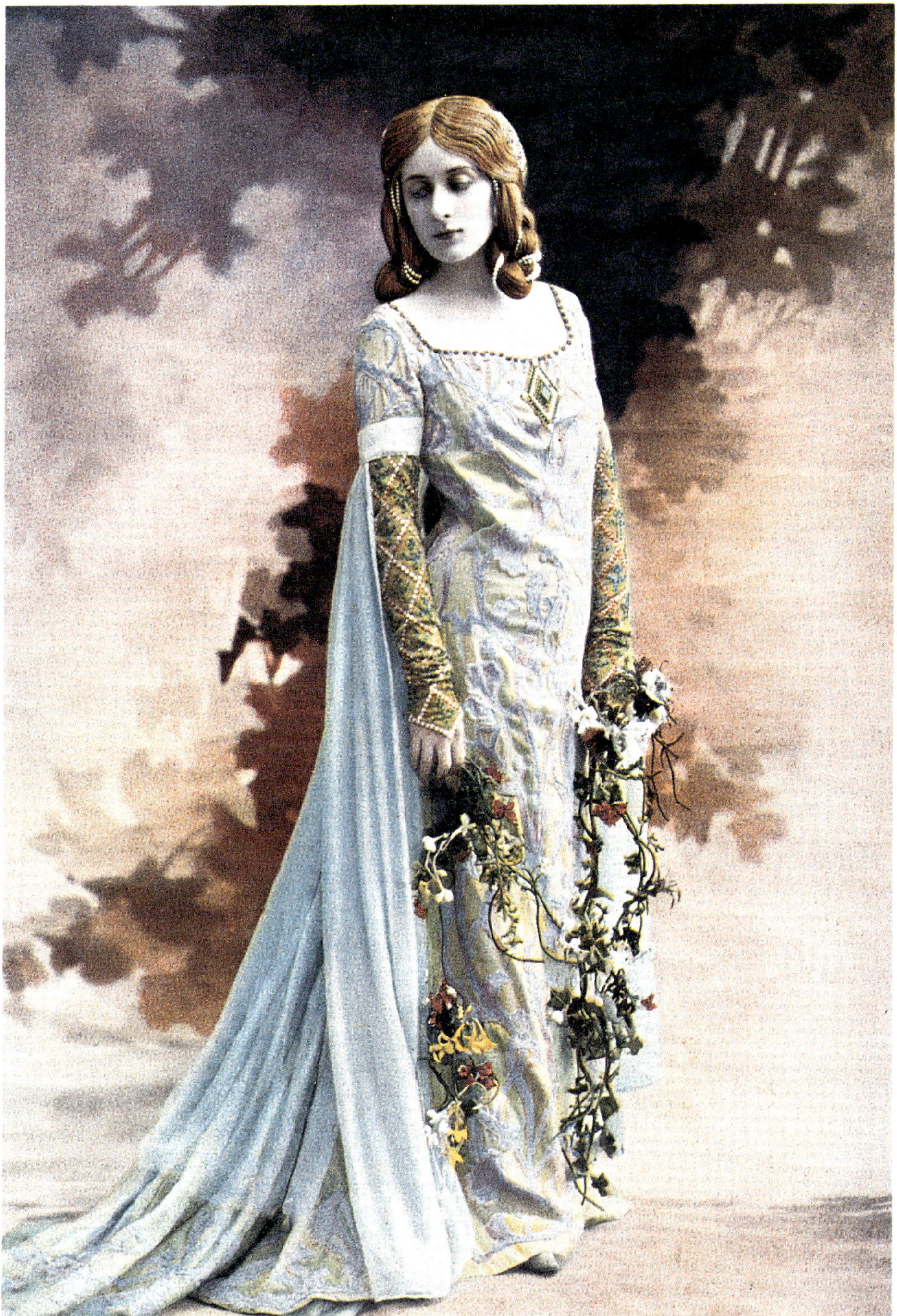

Above: Debussy's first wife, Rosalie Texier, "Lily" or "Lilo," was an unlikely match for the composer. They had few interests in common and Lily was constantly ill. The couple had no children, which may have helped to explain the eventual breakdown of the marriage.

Opposite: Debussy had once intended to be a sailor and always identified with the sea, choosing it as the setting for many of his compositions, as here in the tale of the sirens who appear in mythology.

Marriage to Lily

In her place Claude started a new relationship with Rosalie Texier, who was six years Gaby's junior. Previously Lily, as Debussy called her, had lived with another man and worked as a dressmaker's model and seamstress.

Claude's unmarried liaison with Lily lasted for a year and a half. It seems that he began to enjoy the quiet domesticity of their life together in their new flat in the rue Cardinet. Finally, inspired by the example of his newly wed friend Pierre Louys, he and Lily were married on October 19, 1899. He was thirty-seven, she some ten years younger.

Immediately after the wedding, Claude gave an expensive music lesson (he taught reluctantly when times required it) while the new Madame Debussy waited patiently downstairs in the hall. He spent the money he earned in this way in entertaining Lily, his parents, and his friends at the Brasserie Petit Pousset. The happy pair's honeymoon consisted of a visit to the zoo!

The "Nocturnes"

By this time Debussy had his mind on another, larger project. The *Nocturnes* for orchestra (originally entitled "Evening scenes") were planned in three movements.

The first, "Nuages" – "Clouds" – is one of his most evocative scores. Its shifting strings and plaintive cor anglais evoke a feeling of Paris at dusk. It also echoes the brooding music of *Pelleas,* while the flute patterns also recall the gamelan music of the String Quartet.

"Fetes" is much more lively. After an almost indifferent opening, it constantly changes rhythm and pace, becomes rather jazzy, and then introduces the comic sound of a military brass band (the "Republican Guard") on the march. It soon turns into an orchestral free-for-all, as exciting as Ravel's famous *Bolero.* Then suddenly all this noise dissolves, like a train winding down at the station, or a boat pulling into port.

The third, "Sirenes," has a voiceless women's chorus, which wafts strange sounds on the breeze. Sirens were those birdlike female creatures in Greek mythology whose song lured sailors to their death on the rocks. "The mysterious siren song is heard across waves turned silver with moonlight.
It laughs and fades away,"
wrote Debussy.

Influences

Debussy's interest in music reached far beyond the serious composers of his own time, many of whom he openly expressed disapproval of.

He found inspiration in many places – in medieval Gregorian chant, which he heard at the Paris church of Saint-Gervase; in the works of the great Renaissance composer Palestrina; in the counterpoint of Johann Sebastian Bach. He was increasingly interested in the keyboard works of great composers from Louis XIV's time, such as Couperin and Rameau. He based his suite *Pour le piano* on these earlier composers.

Debussy was also drawn to the much earlier French folksong of the Middle Ages, and especially liked the deep sounding intervals of the fourth and "bare" fifth, known in church music as "organum." This interest became apparent in his settings for choir of poems by the great fifteenth-century prince and poet, Charles, Duke of Orleans.

Debussy's Pleyel upright piano was one of the most precious items in his bachelor apartment, and later in the rue Cardinet, where he lived with his first wife, Lily. A friend once compared the way he played to a mother with her child, cradling it and singing to it softly.

All of these influences helped gradually to open the door to the new "Debussyan" approach to music, which was the result of his search, since student days, for acceptable "new" harmonies and textures – a fresh, original style of his own.

Home life

Claude's life with Lily had developed pleasantly but uneventfully. A quieter, shyer soul than Gaby, she sometimes accompanied him to cafes that Claude had visited with his previous partner.

But she was happiest looking after his simple needs. She kept unwanted strangers from the door so that he might work peacefully, or be permitted to catch up on sleep after working late into the night.

The couple's cats, one of which was named "Line," were Claude's constant companions. They were even allowed to sit on his desk as he composed. Occasionally there was a tragedy when one lost its footing and fell from a high window. But soon another would appear to replace it.

There were also ornamental cats, and Chinese silks, hangings, and carpets gave a cozy feel to the apartment, quite unlike the plainness of the cold attic he had shared with Gaby. Some of these things he bought when a small amount of money came his way. Sometimes, if he liked something, he would put down a deposit and then buy it later, when he could afford it.

A genius at work

Debussy worked very long hours at his Pleyel piano. More than once he thoughtlessly kept others in the next-door apartments awake during the night while he worked enthusiastically at some project, or played his own or another composer's music loudly to friends.

But, despite the happy side to their home life, the relationship with his wife was sometimes strained, especially when Lily suffered a miscarriage. The loss of their child may well have been the prelude to what followed. Sadly, the days of Claude and Lily's marriage were numbered.

"There are no longer any schools of music: the chief task of musicians nowadays is to avoid outside influences."
Claude Debussy, 1908.

Debussy's Pelleas et Melisande *was staged at L'Opera, the old opera house in Paris, one of the best-known musical venues in the world. Many of the most famous nineteenth-century French operas had their first performance either here or at the nearby Opera-Comique.*

Problems and hitches

The premiere of *Pelleas et Melisande* was approaching. The opera had been accepted by the director of the famous Paris Opera-Comique, Albert Carre, and its performance was announced for the forthcoming season of 1901–1902.

Debussy had played the piano score of the opera to both Carre and the conductor, Andre Messager, at his apartment. He now orchestrated it – often revising what he had written – and also helped coach the principal soloists.

The important part of Melisande was allocated to the young Scottish-born soprano Mary Garden. This caused a major disagreement, for Maeterlinck believed that the part had been promised by Debussy to his own girlfriend, Georgette Leblanc. There were several ugly scenes between the author and the composer. Once, Maeterlinck tried to attack Debussy with his walking stick, and later he wrote a bitter letter to the daily paper *Le Figaro* saying he hoped the opera would fail.

There were also many mistakes in the orchestral parts, which Debussy had had copied cheaply. But the main hitch with staging *Pelleas et Melisande* only became clear when the rehearsals were well advanced.

It was then discovered that the many scenery changes required took too long, and Claude was asked to compose several orchestral interludes in a great hurry. Yet when the opera came to be performed on April 30, 1902, it was these hurriedly written interludes that gave it much of its atmosphere.

The premiere of "Pelleas et Melisande"

On the day, many of the people in the audience, especially the students, cheered and clapped wildly to show their approval of Debussy's opera. Others cat-called, and some even booed the gentle death of Melisande. Probably they expected a great dying speech or aria, as was common in opera. One reviewer called it "a work without muscle or bones … an abuse of chromaticism."

But some, like the young writer Jacques Riviere, saw it differently. "Perhaps one cannot imagine just what *Pelleas* meant to the young people aged between sixteen and twenty who took it to their hearts at that first performance. Here was a

In the nineteenth century, operas such as this one in Paris were great social events and attracted huge numbers. The audiences seldom showed restraint in their opinions, and their responses could make or break a composer's career.

wonderful world, a paradise where we could escape from our problems. We escaped there, and the world no longer existed for us."

Where to next?

After *Pelleas et Melisande,* Debussy felt, he said, "like a squeezed lemon, not wanting to learn anything more." He felt that he must move off in a new direction. He could not simply compose another *Pelleas,* even if that was what people wanted. "To repeat oneself is disastrous," he said. "I would rather spend my time growing pineapples!"

Debussy loved Shakespeare. He thought of setting an opera based on Shakespeare's play *As You Like It.* Then he planned some incidental music for a production of *King Lear,* though in fact he composed only two short extracts.

Another writer who attracted Debussy greatly was the American author Edgar Allan Poe, whose weird *Tales of Mystery and Imagination* obsessed many people at the time. He planned a one-act opera based on Poe's story *The Devil in the Belfry,* in which he had the idea that the Devil would whistle on stage, rather than sing. The composer also became interested in another story, *The Fall of the House of Usher*, which was to occupy him to the end of his life.

New piano pieces

But shorter piano pieces were a different matter. In 1903, during a three-month summer vacation in a rented house in Burgundy, close to Lily's parents' home, Claude completed *Estampes.* The word is taken from art, and means "etchings" or "prints."

Each of these three short pieces had an appealing, evocative title. "Pagodes" conjures up visions of splendid Chinese buildings, with the sounds of Oriental gongs and bells.

In "La Soiree dans Granade" – "Evening in Granada" – he made use of an unusual dance rhythm called a "Habanera." This displeased his fellow French composer Ravel, who felt Debussy had copied the idea from one of his own pieces. But

"Music has this over poetry. It can bring together all manner of variations of colour and light."

Claude Debussy.

other musicians welcomed the new piece, finding it evoked the atmosphere of Spain.

The third piece in the set was entitled "Jardins sous la pluie" – "Gardens in the Rain." All three were premiered by the talented young pianist Ricardo Vines, who now began to give first performances of many of Debussy's works.

Recognition and deceit

Early in 1903, Debussy, still aged only forty, received formal recognition. The French government appointed him a "Chevalier of the Legion of Honour," a knighthood. He was pleased to accept it, he said, for the sake of his proud old parents, after all the sacrifices they had made for him.

But the following year was a fateful one for Debussy. His relationship with Lily was getting dull. Sometimes she was suspicious of his unexplained absences, and there were arguments.

During this time Claude saw more and more of a rich society woman who was soon to change his life. She was Emma Bardac, a capable singer and the mother of one his pupils, Raoul Bardac.

Debussy, seen in one of the few pictures with his parents, was a typical example of a talented child who came from a fairly modest or humble background. Without the advantage of wealth, he had to struggle to make his way in the early days before he became successful.

Both Claude and Lily were invited to dinner at the Bardacs' house, and Debussy visited Emma more and more to join in musical sessions and soirees, or to accompany her on the piano. It was almost as if he had rediscovered Madame Vasnier.

By the next year his interest in Emma had become a fixation, and finally a passion. No matter that she was married – her husband, Monsieur Sigismonde Bardac, was many years older. He was a wealthy financier, and was often absent for long periods.

Emma's affections were also now concentrated on Claude. They were the same age. Her children, Raoul and Dolly, liked him too.

The joyous isle

Finally, in the summer of 1904, the pair "eloped." Emma and Claude went to the pretty island of Jersey, off the French coast, where they stayed in an elegant hotel, and enjoyed the sea and the fresh air and the feelings of being in love.

That year was one of the happiest times of Debussy's life. His inspiration returned, and he recorded it by completing one of the most cheerful piano pieces he had ever written – *L'Isle joyeuse* – The Island of Joy.

By contrast, Debussy's song-cycle, *Fetes galantes*, included one of his saddest songs – "Colloque sentimental." It tells of a meeting between two ghosts whose love is over and forgotten.

With these songs and the new *Masques* for piano, Claude's developing style finally matured. He at last seemed to find his own voice, the one he had been searching for ever since *Pelleas*.

All the techniques with which Debussy had experimented over the years, those very things Conservatoire students had always been taught not to use, he now felt free to use unashamedly.

In the idyllic hideaway of Jersey, Debussy felt able to work for the first time in a long while. The beauty of his surroundings and the companionship of his latest love, Emma Bardac, brought him peace of mind.

Below and opposite: A recent picture of the Grand Hotel at Eastbourne, on the English south coast. Debussy spent some of his happiest moments by the sea for which he had a deep respect, once comparing its sound to that of music.

As well as the unusual chords he had experimented with in early years, Debussy made frequent use of the "pentatonic" scale, a simple pattern found particularly in folk music, which uses only five notes.

Then there was the "whole-tone" scale, which rises by tones only – making seven notes in the octave, not the usual eight. There were also the many unusual scales or "modes," with their sad or bright moods, which he had learned from playing the works of Russian composers like Borodin and Balakirev, and also from his later exploration of Mussorgsky.

Perhaps most important of all was his bold use of unusual intervals and chords, utilizing all twelve notes of the chromatic scale.

Debussy's music was not merely revolutionary – it was a completely new form of "Classicism." More and more he worked toward perfecting a pure Classical style and system of his own, using his own novel harmonic ideas.

He spent literally hours planning every bar and every chord, so that each idea and every harmony would appear in what he judged *exactly* the right order. Single-handed, Debussy moved music's goalposts. He changed the rules.

In effect, he launched twentieth-century music.

A messy marriage break-up

When he and Emma returned to Paris later that year, Claude left Lily for good, at the same time losing some of his close friends who did not approve of his actions. He moved out of their apartment, leaving her alone at the rue Cardinet, and rented an apartment in the avenue d'Alphand.

Emma applied for a divorce, and a little over a year later, once both divorces had been granted, the couple moved to a house in the avenue du Bois de Boulogne. It was to be Debussy's home for the rest of his life.

Lily, distraught at losing her husband, shot herself with a pistol. She failed to kill herself, but the newspapers soon heard about it and this led to a great scandal.

Despite doubts about his own suitability for family life, Debussy's second marriage, to Emma Bardac, gave him a secure home and a child. The marriage lasted through his illness and darker periods, until the composer's death.

Claude and Emma had to delay their marriage until the news of his own divorce had been confirmed. It was an unpleasant time for all concerned.

With a well-to-do marriage lined-up and *Pelleas* running successfully at the Opera-Comique – it soon achieved one hundred performances – Claude, now aged forty-three, should have at last had the prospect of some security and even wealth.

These hopes disappeared. Worries about money, plus the hectic work schedules and performing that took him all over the globe in order to earn a living, soon broke his health.

Luckily help was at hand. Jacques Durand had agreed to become his regular publisher, taking all his new and some old works, and paying him one thousand francs per month – double what the kindly Hartmann used to pay him.

"The Sea"

That summer of 1905, as soon as both divorces had been heard in court, Claude and Emma took off for England. They stayed in the famous Grand Hotel at Eastbourne, by the sea. And it was there that Debussy put the finishing touches on one of his most famous works of all, *La Mer – The Sea*.

He had loved the sea all his life. As a small boy, he had gazed in wonder at the sea off the coast of Cannes. "In a storm at sea," he once said, "you realize you're really alive."

The surge and swell of the sea and its many intricate patterns have inspired many composers including Debussy, who used it as the subject for one of his most famous pieces, La Mer.

"*The sound of the sea, the curve of a horizon, wind in leaves, the cry of a bird leave manifold impressions in us. And suddenly, without our wishing it at all, one of these memories spills from us and finds expression in musical language.*"

Claude Debussy, 1911.

Now Debussy, the brilliant orchestrator, poured all those strong feelings onto paper. *La Mer* is one of the most remarkable pieces ever composed for orchestra. It is a work full of light and movement, often stormy, yet sometimes contrastingly serene, with great tunes and melodies that begin to build, like the waves of the sea, and then disperse just as quickly into tiny patterns and fragments.

Its rhythms are often very complex. Yet the result is a wonderful symphonic poem – indeed, almost a symphony – a seascape full of sudden tension and excitement and release.

Its three movements – "From dawn to midday on the sea," "Wave-games" (full of those tiny motifs and "arabesques" of which Debussy was so fond), and "Dialogue of the wind and the sea" (he marked this "energetic and stormy") – sweep audiences off their feet. Today it is one of his best-known works. It has been widely recorded and is played in every major concert hall in the world.

Debussy's self-imposed "rules" remained very much his own. Some people believe they can detect carefully worked-out calculations in *La Mer* that relate to the famous "golden mean," a technical device used to achieve perfect proportions in art. Debussy gave as much attention to these details as a painter or architect would.

"What gave [Debussy] more genuine pleasure than anything else was to listen to his adorable little daughter Chouchou talking or singing, playing the piano, or dancing to some tune he had composed specially."
Pasteur Vallery-Radot.

A sometimes happy family

This was a very memorable year for Emma and Claude in another way. On October 30, 1905, soon after the move to their new home, and only two weeks after the premiere of *La Mer* in Paris, Emma gave birth to a daughter.

She was called Claude-Emma, after her two parents, but all her life she was known as "Chouchou" – "pet," or "darling."

Chouchou Debussy was a clever girl, who grew up looking the image of her father and was undoubtedly the apple of his eye.

Claude and Emma had been unable to marry while their divorces were pending. Now at last they were able to, and in the same year as the birth of their daughter, at their local Town Hall registry office, they dedicated their lives to each other.

Claude-Emma – "Chouchou" – Debussy's daughter, was a great source of happiness for the composer, and she was reputedly the only person toward whom he showed any emotion. Tragically, she survived her father by only one year, dying at the age of thirteen in the postwar epidemic of diphtheria.

45

But a new gloom and resentment was already beginning to fill their lives. The rapture and excitement of Jersey had given way to the plain routines of "bourgeois" domestic life. Claude appeared to be impossible to please. Even at this late stage, he seems to have had marriage doubts.

"I am writing between attacks of joy and sadness," he confided to others. "Peace doesn't dwell in my soul. Is it the landscape of this part of town? Or that I am not made to put up with domestic life?" In short, Claude was never satisfied. It was part of his nature.

"Images"

But there were other reasons for his restlessness, too. His creative urge had returned. On the best days, he was positively teeming with ideas. The year after the birth of Chouchou, he composed a set of three *Images* for piano. Two of them – "Reflections on the water" and "Homage to Rameau" – were very atmospheric, serene, and stately, while the last – "Movement" – is a carefree, fast-flowing toccata, a rapid movement full of lightning flashes of brilliance and conflicting rhythms.

A second set of *Images* for piano soon followed. These included the deep, resounding bell-effects of "Cloches a travers les feuilles" – "Bells through the leaves" and "Poissons d'or" – "Goldfish" – a work full of darting and dazzling effects. The latter was said to be inspired by a picture from his study – a pretty Chinese lacquered panel in black, inlaid in gold and mother-of-pearl, which showed a scene of a fish flickering through the water.

But the name *Images* was to become more famous still. *Images pour orchestre* was Claude's first major composition for orchestra since *La Mer*. It cost him much hard work.

The best known of these three *Images* is "Iberia," which itself also consists of three sections. Debussy's love of triple, or ternary, form seems to have excelled itself here.

"Iberia" is full of castanets and tambourines, echoing the Moorish rhythms from southern Spain. The focus of the piece, "Les parfums de la nuit," is

---

"None among the younger, or older, composers is endowed with a melodic inventiveness that is more enticing, more subtle, more discriminating. And moreover, none of them uses harmonies that are more original, more refined, or more subtle."

P. Lalo, *from* Le Temps.

one of Debussy's loveliest works. It evokes the "intoxicating spell" of Andalusian nights, full of evening fragrance and dreamlike charm.

Laughter and anxiety

To celebrate Chouchou's birth, Debussy had been writing a charming piano piece called "Serenade for a doll." Now he composed a new suite for piano, *Children's Corner,* which was played in public for the first time in December 1908.

It was Chouchou's toys that inspired these famous piano pieces. *Children's Corner* is quite difficult to play. Yet this is Debussy at his most clever and lighthearted – the lively, irreverent entertainer whom his friends remembered from younger days.

"Jimbo's Lullaby" introduces Chouchou's toy elephant, who clumsily lurches into everything around him. "The Snow Is Dancing" suggests a sad, dreary day in the nursery when there's nothing to do and you aren't allowed out to play. "Golliwog's Cakewalk" converts a band tune Claude once heard in London into a jazzy ragtime. In it, he even "sends up" a theme from his own best-loved opera, *Tristan and Isolde.*

Such frivolity, however, soon became mixed with concern. Early in 1909, Claude suffered serious bleeding, which required immediate treatment. He was in considerable pain. It was the first evidence, though poor Debussy did not know it at the time, of the rectal cancer that was to make his last years a misery.

Debussy the critic

As the year progressed, Debussy, now aged forty-seven, was finally persuaded to become a member of the Conseil Superieur, or Council of the Conservatoire. It was something he had always previously resisted, remembering his own difficult days as a student there. But from now on, he attended its meetings regularly until only a few weeks before his death.

Yet Debussy was still a controversial figure in

Despite early signs of the illness that was to take his life, Debussy, pictured here in 1910, was at the summit of his fame. He completed his set of twenty-four piano Preludes *in 1913, into which he was to pack many of the original and innovative musical ideas that had obsessed him from student days.*

French musical circles. Not long before, he had written a series of articles for two Paris journals, in which he disguised his own sharply critical opinions by attributing them to a fictional character that he invented, called "Monsieur Croche," which means "Mr. Quaver" or "Mr. Cross."

His articles were often sarcastic and even hostile, and since he attacked the works of many composers, they made him plenty of enemies. But Debussy was an informed and perceptive critic. The best of his articles shed light on music of many periods, from the medieval period to his own day.

Twenty-four "Preludes"

This perceptivity was instrumental in the development of Debussy's own highly original style. His ingenious ideas about how to write for the piano finally came to fruition in his two books of twelve *Preludes,* the first of which was published in 1910. All of his composing genius is on show in these twenty-four brilliantly varied pieces, many of which are only three or four minutes long.

An orchestral concert in Paris at the Salle Pleyel, named after the famous French composer and piano maker, Ignaz Pleyel. Debussy wrote extensively for the piano, although his wider recognition rests on his orchestral works.

"Minstrels" and "The Dance of Puck" have the same kind of gaiety as "Golliwog's Cakewalk." "The Sunken Cathedral," with its progressions of chords, rising and falling like a huge arch, is an impressive piece – powerful and resonant.

"Footsteps in the Snow" and "The Girl with the Flaxen Hair" are more delicate and reflective. "What the West Wind Saw" is light and fast. "The Hills of Anacapri," one of the most joyous of all, makes use of boisterous Italian tunes from Naples, while "The Interrupted Serenade" includes a brilliant parody of Spanish guitar music.

There is no point in looking for the title at the beginning of each *Prelude*. Debussy printed them at the end, mainly because he wanted them to be treated as works of music in their own right, regardless of any visual association.

Some of the second set of *Preludes*, published four years later – such as "Fog," with its quick changes of time – are tricky for any young pianist to play. The final *Prelude*, "Fireworks," makes a sparkling finale to these imaginative piano pieces.

A project that failed

In the meantime, Debussy had been continuing work on his one-act opera, *The Fall of the House of Usher* – first the libretto, and then the music, in two scenes. The Metropolitan Opera House in New York even paid him a modest sum for first performance rights to both his two projected "Poe" operas. (The other was *The Devil in the Belfry*.) This might later have made him a rich man, so it is especially tragic that Debussy never completed either part of his operatic "double bill."

The Fall of the House of Usher is a gloomy story about a brother and sister who are living out their years in a huge, ghostly mansion. The story was ideally suited to Debussy's style and variable moods. But instead of writing it at speed, remembering the success of his rapidly composed interludes for *Pelleas et Melisande*, he gradually became more and more enmeshed in its dark nature. The gloomy *House of Usher* came to dominate his life.

"In opera there is always too much singing. Music should be as swift and mobile as the words themselves."

Claude Debussy.

The Martyrdom of Saint Sebastian *is one of Debussy's surprisingly neglected works, although by the 1990s it had become more widely recognized. The original performance was badly received and this obscured the real quality of the music.*

The music that has survived, in sketches, suggests a highly atmospheric but claustrophobic opera, a worthy follow-up to *Pelleas et Melisande* – a mysterious, though also deeply pessimistic, modern stage work. Though some parts have been orchestrated, it was never completed.

"[Debussy] was extremely sensitive to the opinions of a few, but supremely indifferent to the favours of the crowd."

Raymond Bonheur.

Saints and martyrs

Instead, Claude turned to other projects. He was approached by the Italian poet Gabriele d'Annunzio for music to accompany a play about a Christian martyr from Roman times, Saint Sebastian, who was killed with many arrows for his faith.

D'Annunzio's play fancifully linked the story of Saint Sebastian with a beautiful Greek god, Adonis, who was said to have died and been resurrected. In it, the part of the saint was played by a female dancer.

The play caused quite an uproar. The Archbishop of Paris declared it blasphemous, and threatened to excommunicate Catholics who went to see it.

Le Martyre de Saint Sebastien breathes the spirit of Wagner's last opera and ends in a blaze of glorious light. Sadly, the play was soon overshadowed by the Paris premiere of Stravinsky's dazzling ballet *Petrushka*. But Debussy's lovely music – even though far too rarely heard today – lives on in some fine recordings.

Stravinsky

Igor Stravinsky was the rising musical star of the Ballets Russes, a brilliant Russian touring dance company managed by Serge Diaghilev. Debussy admired Stravinsky and his music, even though he knew that the younger man's reputation was growing at the expense of his own. It was a case of the old revolutionary meeting the new.

Together they spent a highly enjoyable day playing through the early drafts of Stravinsky's new ballet, *The Rite of Spring* – a remarkable feat of sight-reading by Debussy, who managed to play the difficult rhythms of the lower part.

Diaghilev also admired Debussy's music, and was eager to have a new ballet from him. At first, reluctantly, Claude agreed to allow a staging of his *Prelude a 'l'Apres-midi d'un faune,'* choreographed by the ballet's brilliant leading dancer, Vaclav Nijinsky.

Debussy was never really happy with this staged version of his famous work. Nijinsky's erotic performance brought

The new kind of free-flowing style and use of Eastern influences in Debussy's Prelude a 'l'Apres-midi d'un faune' *gave plenty of opportunity for experimentation in costume design for the ballet.*

Debussy had little respect for Nijinsky's ballet of his Prelude a 'l'Apres-midi d'un faune,' calling it ugly and peculiar. Its sensuality shocked many of the audience.

out the sex and sensuality, but seems to have lacked the subtle suggestiveness of both the music and Mallarme's fragrant poem. It caused momentary outrage among Paris audiences, but was rapidly overtaken by Ravel's ballet *Daphnis et Chloe,* premiered only a week later.

Critics were quick to point this out. One even suggested that musicians of the younger generation like Ravel could compose "Debussyan" music better than Debussy himself!

"Jeux"

Finally, when Diaghilev doubled his fee, the reluctant Claude was persuaded to compose a work especially for the Ballets Russes. The new ballet was called *Jeux*. The choreography was once again devised by Nijinsky.

Jeux depicts a game of tennis which takes place in a "fantastically lit" garden, with three players – a young man and two girls. The loss of a tennis ball leads to a series of *pas de deux,* or exchanges and courtship games played between all three characters.

At the end, an unseen fourth hand throws in a ball. Who can it be? The young man and girls are surprised and frightened, and run away.

Almost forgotten

Debussy's fragmented score for *Jeux* is one of the most subtle and ingenious he had composed since *La Mer*. But for a long time its great merits were forgotten. Its performance in 1913 was eclipsed yet again by a Stravinsky premiere – this time that of the ballet *The Rite of Spring*.

A few wise conductors helped keep the memory of the piece alive by playing it to audiences, until the influential French composer and conductor Pierre Boulez drew fresh attention to its extraordinary inventiveness almost half a century later.

But one tiny work from this period does survive as one of the most beautiful of all Debussy's smaller pieces. *Syrinx* is an evocative medium for solo flute. Its flowing "roulades," or rising and falling patterns, often recall the *Prelude a 'l'Apres-midi d'un faune.'*

Last songs

Debussy also returned to song-writing. Recently he had completed a beautifully wistful set of songs called *Le Promenoir des deux amants – The Lovers Promenade* – based on a sixteenth-century text. Now Claude turned to the works of the famous medieval French poet Francois Villon, who was also known as a bit of a rogue.

Debussy's songs were entitled *Three Ballads of Francois Villon*. What a contrast they make! "Prayer to the Mother of God" is gentle and repectful, while "The Ballad of the Women of Paris," with its list of desirable ladies and courtesans from bygone times, is one of the "raciest" texts ever set to music!

Lastly, Claude composed a set of songs to words by his old friend Mallarme. Their high-riding vocal line looks back to some of his early songs, while the piano part is full of those technical devices familiar in his maturer style.

Following page: Rome was just one of the places Debussy visited before World War I in order to conduct and promote his music, and to earn some much-needed money to enable the family to maintain its lifestyle. Generally, however, he much preferred to stay in the familiar surroundings of Paris.

"To finish a work, isn't it a bit like the death of someone one loves?"
Claude Debussy, January 1895.

Travels and triumphs

Claude and Emma were again short of money. To earn more, Debussy had to travel. Sadly, his poor health and Emma's concern prevented him from visiting the United States, where he might have made a lot of money. But he made working trips to Austria and Hungary, conducting in Vienna and playing the piano in Budapest, and Holland.

He also returned to some of the places he had known in his youth. He was warmly welcomed in Russia, visiting St. Petersburg and Moscow, where he met his old friend, Sophie von Meck, now grown up and married. And he was wildly acclaimed in Rome – the very city where he had felt so lonely and homesick all those years ago.

War

In 1914, war finally broke out in Europe. Germany invaded France on August 3, and many families were evacuated from Paris, including the Debussys.

They went briefly to Angers on the Loire river, staying there in safety

Debussy's life, like that of many others, was made miserable by war. The rue de Rivoli, one of Paris's most fashionable streets, was among the many areas hit by German shelling.

until the front line stabilized after the French won a victory at the Marne – the very river where Debussy, Chausson, and their friends had spent many hours boating together at Luzancy in happier times.

The war was not the only thing that depressed Claude. His mother died the following March, and Emma too lost her mother soon after. Furthermore, some rivals were trying to stop him from being elected a fellow of the leading artistic body in Paris, the Academie des Beaux Arts. "The door of the Academy must at all costs be barred against a man capable of such atrocities," wrote Saint-Saens, one of Debussy's bitterest conservative opponents, referring hostilely to what he saw as the composer's obvious disregard for musical tradition.

Finding a cause

Yet these lean wartime years were in a sense the start of a new creative period for Debussy.

As the people in Paris suffered shortages and personal losses, he was lured away from his gloomy home in the Bois de Boulogne. So often the "outsider," Debussy seemed to yearn for more popular recognition as a national figure. He said he wanted to be described as a *musicien francais* – a musician of France. He took part in concerts in aid of war veterans and played a new role in helping cheer others. He even composed an "Ode to France."

Perhaps most poignantly of all, Claude was deeply saddened by the death of a young friend in battle. He wrote a piece for two pianos, *En blanc et noir – Black and White* – and dedicated the slow second movement to this young fallen French soldier.

Last flowering

There were other important tasks. Debussy was asked by his publisher to edit the piano works of Chopin, who had lived in Paris when his own homeland, Poland, was occupied by foreign powers, just as France was in 1914.

Claude devoted long hours to this important work. The edition was soon ready; the experience of editing Chopin's works gave him new energy. Inspired, he quickly set to work on his own series of piano *Etudes,* or *Studies.*

Finally, Debussy began a set of instrumental sonatas. Writing these gave him a chance to bring a new economy of form to his instrumental writing. He planned a series of six, but only three were completed before his death.

The first, the Cello Sonata, has a restrained, Classical feel. The second, for an attractive combination of flute, viola, and harp, is a cheerful piece, and much more lush and sensual.

But it is the Violin Sonata, his last important completed work, with its sad "Oriental" character, which strikes the deepest note, and seemed to point a way forward for Debussy, had he survived the war.

Decline

"I am writing like a madman, or as one who knows he must die in the morning," Debussy wrote to a friend, as though he knew his fate.

Debussy's illness had become worse, and before Christmas 1915 he had undergone an operation for

"Life has become too hard and Claude Debussy, writing no more music, has no longer any reason to exist. I have no hobbies, they never taught me anything but music."

Claude Debussy, 1916.

rectal cancer. Nonetheless he kept working on his last opera – *The Fall of the House of Usher*.

Emma, whose own health was not always good, did what she could to keep his spirits up. He continued to attend the meetings of the Council of the Academy throughout the war, and abandoned them only a few weeks before his death.

In 1916, Debussy had to undergo radium treatment (still a fairly new discovery) and underwent a second operation. With his energy sapped by morphine injections to lessen the pain, he lost the will and the urge to work. He was a poor shadow of himself. "I feel like a walking corpse," he said. Friends noticed that his face was thin and drawn.

Debussy's Violin Sonata, which has a passionate urgency about it in the finale, was the composer's last completed work. He accompanied the first public performance in 1917 and again in St.-Jean-de-Luz, only a few months before he died.

The struggle ends

Claude rallied a little the next summer. He even accompanied a friend in performing the new Violin Sonata in public.

But by the end of 1917, his illness was worse. He now had to lie down all the time, and took to his bed. One of his most loyal friends, the pianist Ricardo

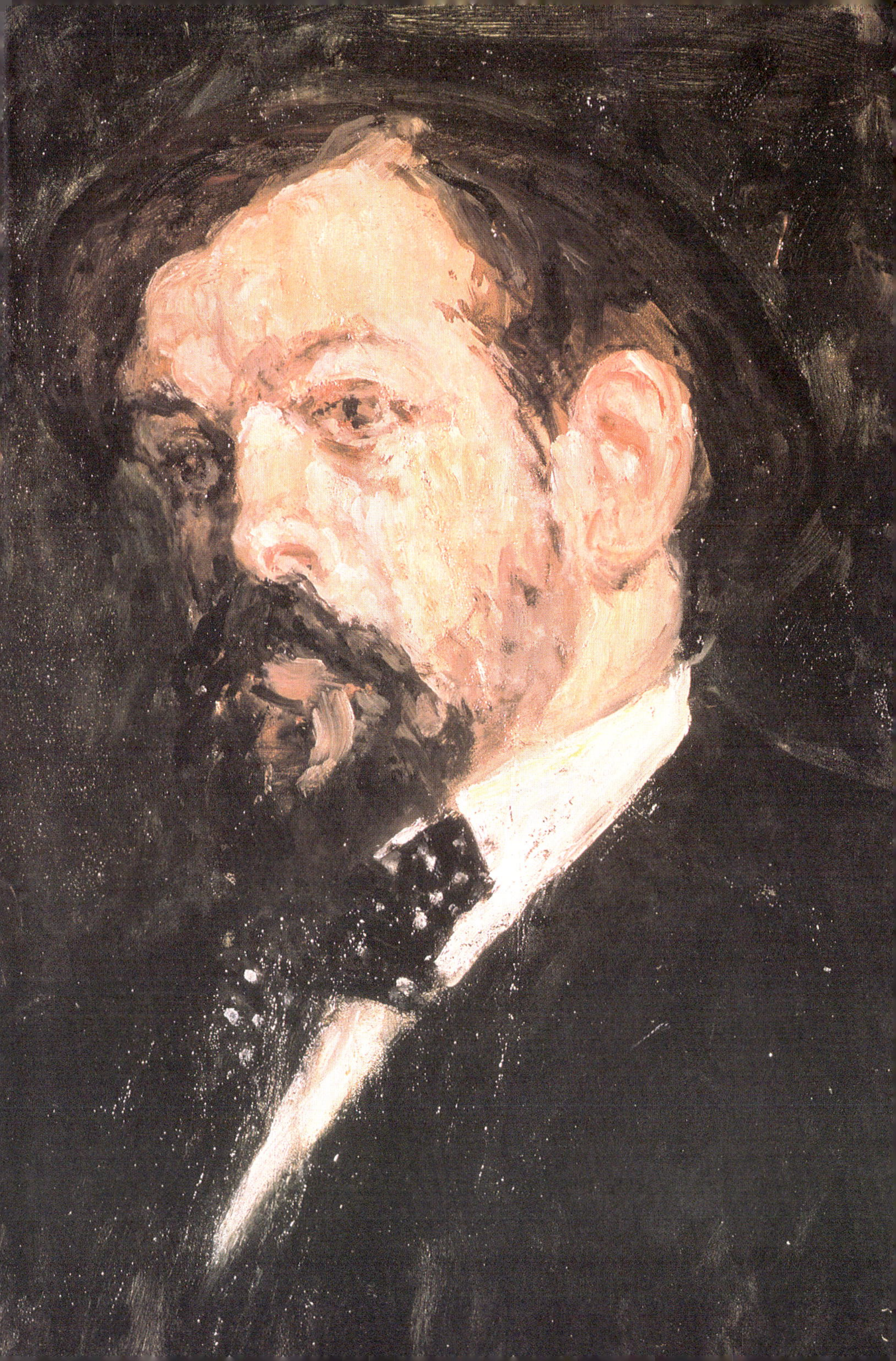

It took nine years for Debussy to compose Pelleas et Melisande *which was the culmination of all he had written before. Although widely declaimed at the time, it has since become known as the central work of his life, through which he hoped to "Liberate dramatic music from the heavy yoke it has been wearing for so long."*

"Although [Debussy's] output was relatively small, he freed music from the restraints of traditional forms, such as the symphony and sonata, in favour of pieces inspired by poems, moods, and landscapes; and by using unusual scales and harmonies to loosen the shackles of major and minor keys, Debussy paved the way for a vast range of experiments in twentieth-century music."

Wendy Thompson, from Claude Debussy.

Vines, came to play the *Etudes* to the poor composer as he lay there, incapacitated and dying.

The end came on March 25, 1918. With Claude and Emma were just a few close friends. At last, at around ten o'clock, Debussy died. It was a cruel day. German shells were exploding in Paris, some even landing near his house.

Debussy's influence

There is virtually no composer of the twentieth century who has not been influenced in some way by Debussy. His harmonies, his new approach to structuring musical works, his use of chromaticism and unusual scales, and his subtle use of the orchestra are just a few of the ways in which he made a difference to just about every major composer who followed him.

Stravinsky, Ravel, Bartok, Messiaen, Stockhausen, and Boulez are just a few of the names on whom Debussy's music has had a crucial, lasting influence. More important, it was his courage that inspired many others, from his own generation to younger composers of the present day, to go ahead courageously, to make their *own* patterns and follow their own inclinations.

Courage and boldness have been the key to twentieth-century modernism in the arts. In music, we perhaps owe that more to Claude Debussy than to anyone else – the rebel who not only changed the "rules," but did away with them forever.

Important dates

1862   Aug. 22: Achille Claude Debussy is born to Manuel-Achille and Victorine Debussy at St. Germain-en-Laye, near Paris.

1871   Debussy meets Madame Maute de Fleurville and begins piano lessons with her in Paris.

1872   Oct.: Debussy, aged ten, enters the Paris Conservatoire. He studies solfege under Albert Lavignac and the piano under Antoine Marmontel.

1880   Debussy meets Madame Nadezhda von Meck and becomes tutor to her children. In Paris, Debussy enters the composition class of Ernest Guiraud.

1881   Debussy becomes friendly with Madame Vasnier and visits the von Mecks in Russia during the summer.

1884   Debussy, aged twenty-one, gains the Prix de Rome.

1885   Jan.: Debussy begins study at the Villa Medici, Rome. He meets the composer and piano virtuoso Franz Liszt, who becomes an important inspiration to the younger musician.

1887   Debussy finishes outlining the orchestral work *Printemps*.

1888   Debussy completes a new choral work, *La Damoiselle elue*.

1889   Debussy's *Petite Suite*, for piano, is published and performed.

1890   Debussy begins to compose his *Suite bergamasque* for piano, including the famous "Clair de lune," and to work on his uncompleted opera, *Rodrigue et Chimene*. He meets Gabrielle Dupont – "Gaby."

1891   Debussy meets the composer Erik Satie, who becomes a lifelong friend.

1893   Dec. 29: The first performance of Debussy's String Quartet is well received.

1894   Feb.: Debussy becomes engaged to the young singer Therese Roger. The engagement is soon broken off.
Dec. 22: Debussy's orchestral work, *Prelude a 'l'Apres-midi d'un faune,'* is performed at the Societe Nationale to enthusiastic public response.

1895   Aug.: Debussy completes the first version of his opera *Pelleas et Melisande*.

1899   Oct. 19: Debussy marries Rosalie Texier – "Lily," a dressmaker.

1900   Oct. 27: Debussy's orchestral work *Nocturnes* is performed to high acclaim.

1902   Jan. 11: The suite *Pour le piano* is given its first performance.
April 30: The first performance of Debussy's opera *Pelleas et Melisande* creates a scandal.

1903   Debussy composes the piano pieces *Estampes* and is appointed Chevalier of the Legion of Honour, equivalent to a knighthood.

1904   June: Debussy composes the second set of *Fetes galantes*, *L'Isle joyeuse*, and the new *Masques* for piano.
The composer leaves his wife for Emma Bardac. Lily attempts suicide. Debussy begins work on his orchestral work *La Mer*.

1905   Aug.: Debussy divorces his first wife and marries Madame Bardac.
Oct. 15: The first performance of *La Mer*.
Oct. 30: Debussy's daughter, Claude-Emma – "Chouchou" – is born.

1908	Debussy completes *Children's Corner,* for piano, inspired by Chouchou's toys.
1909	Debussy becomes afflicted with cancer. He is appointed member of the council of the Conservatoire.
1910	Debussy's first book of twelve *Preludes* for piano is published.
1911	Debussy's *Le Martyre de Saint Sebastien* is staged.
1912	Nijinsky produces a ballet based on *Prelude a 'l'Apres-midi d'un faune,'* which does not meet with Debussy's approval. However, he collaborates with the dancer on *Jeux* for Diaghilev's Ballets Russes.
1915	Debussy composes the Cello Sonata, *En blanc et noir,* and the piano *Etudes.* Debussy undergoes an operation and his health begins to deteriorate.
1916	Debussy undergoes further surgery and receives radium treatment. He finishes his last completed work – the Violin Sonata.
1918	March 25: Debussy dies, aged fifty-five.

Recommended Listening

Suite bergamasque – "Clair de lune" is a very atmospheric piano piece. The music, as implied by the title, gives the impression of a still, moonlit night and requires that the pianist plays very delicately.

Prelude a 'l'Apres-midi d'un faune' – In this piece, Debussy tried to capture the dreamy and mysterious atmosphere of the poem on which it was based. In it, a mythical creature lies dreaming in the forest, in the heat of a summer's afternoon. The solo flute opens the piece with a calm, floating melody. This is followed by distant horncalls and the harp.

"Fetes" from *Nocturnes* – Debussy aimed to capture the impression of a festival in this piece. It opens with a happy dance followed by a brass fanfare. As the music develops, it becomes more vigorous with much use of percussion.

Pelleas et Melisande – Debussy's only completed opera, one of his finest achievements, whose unusual orchestral and vocal writing amounted to a revolutionary fresh approach to serious opera.

La Mer – Debussy's three-movement orchestral work depicting the sea in all its moods, both angry and serene, and in which he uses many of the devices characteristic of the compositional style he developed in the early 1900s.

Preludes, Book I – in these twelve piano pieces Debussy uses the full range of the novel ideas he had been exploring since his student days, especially unusual chords, scales, intervals and musical forms. He added a picturesque title at the *end* of each piece.

Syrinx – This piece for solo flute is very unusual, since it has no accompaniment. It contains some difficult fast passages and uses influences from the East.

Jeux – This was Debussy's last major orchestral work. He wrote it as a ballet score. The whole piece is made up of tiny fragments of melody thrown between various instruments. It makes very subtle use of the percussion and the celeste (a small keyboard instrument which uses bells instead of strings to produce the sound.)

Glossary

Arabesque: A type of ornamental melody.
Aria: An elaborate song for solo voice, usually forming part of a larger work, such as an *opera*.
Cantata: An extended piece of choral music with orchestral accompaniment. It can be either religious or non religious, and with or without solo voices.
Castanets: A percussion instrument, originating from Spain and made from two pieces of hollow wood which are struck together.
Chromatic: Involving the sharpening or flattening of notes, or having notes other than those used in a *diatonic* scale. The chromatic scale consists of twelve notes and includes all the white and black notes on a keyboard.
Classical: A style in art, literature, and music popular between about 1750 and 1810. The characteristics of Classicism are elegance, clear shape, and balance.
Concerto: A composition, usually in three movements, for a solo instrument, supported by an orchestra.
Ensemble: A group of singers or instruments playing together.
Folk music: A composition based on folklore, or unwritten stories, customs, and legends handed down from generation to generation and attached to a particular group of people.
Gamelan: An orchestra of Eastern Asian origin which uses some stringed and woodwind instruments, but is mostly made up of percussion instruments.
Gregorian chant: A type of plainsong.
Harmony: A combination of musical notes played simultaneously, forming a chord. The term has come to signify the production of a pleasing sound or *tone*.
Incidental: Music composed to accompany a play.
Interlude: A piece of music that is played between scenes of a dramatic performance.
Interval: The difference of pitch between two notes.
Jazz: A style of music characterized by its strong rhythms and improvised *melodies*.
Key: The scale (a progression of notes in order of pitch, or sound of a note in a specific scale) that the composer has chosen for a particular piece of music or *melody*.
Libretto: The words that are set to music in an *opera*.
Melody: A succession of musical notes that make up a tune within a piece of music.
Motif: A musical theme or fragment used by a composer to represent a particular idea, person, or thing.
Opera: A dramatic work in which all or most of the performers sing their parts.
Orchestration: The arrangement, by instruments, of a piece of music to be played by an orchestra.
Patron/ess: A person who gives financial support to an artist or cause they feel is deserving.
Piano trio: An *ensemble* of players – piano, violin, and cello. The name refers to the players and also to the music they play.
Pleyel piano: A type of piano named after an Austrian-born nineteenth-century piano maker and composer.
Radical: A person who looks for extreme change in the circumstances around them.
Ragtime: A type of jazz music with a syncopated or jagged rhythm.
Romantic: A style in music, literature, and art that was characteristic of the period between about 1810 and 1900. The music was often emotional and dramatic, using freer or more expanded forms than those used by earlier *Classical* composers.
Semitone: The smallest interval between two musical notes in a scale. Two semitones make a *tone*.
Score: A master copy of a piece of music, showing all the parts of each instrument. The instruments are always written in the same order down the page.
Soiree: An evening social gathering, usually in a private house, where guests are entertained by music.
Sonata: A musical composition, usually for solo piano or for a solo instrument with piano accompaniment. It also refers to a form or structure employed in symphonic works.
Sonorous: In music, a resonant or loud and rich sound.
Soprano: The highest female singing voice.
Suite: A set of musical compositions related in some way and usually intended to be performed together in a sequence.
Symphonic poem: A piece of music based on a piece of writing such as a folktale, usually telling a story or describing a character.
Symphony: A large-scale piece of music, usually in several movements, for orchestra. The first movement traditionally uses a *sonata* form.
Tone: A musical sound or pitch; or an interval consisting of two *semitones*.
Virtuoso: A musical performer with remarkable skill and technical expertise.

Index

D'Annunzio, Gabriele 50-51

Bach, Johann Sebastian 34
Banville, Theodore de 17, 24
Bardac, Emma 39-40, 42-43, 45, 56, 58, 60
Baudelaire, Charles 21
Botticelli, Alessandro 18
Boulez, Pierre 53, 60
Burne-Jones, Edward 21

Chausson, Ernest 21
Chopin, Frederic 10, 57
Classicism 42

Debussy
  Achille, Claude
    birth of 7
    childhood 8, 10
    compositions of
      choral
        Diane au bois 17, 25
        L'Enfant prodigue 15
        Le Gladiateur 15
        Zuleima 17
      operas and stage works
        La Damoiselle elue 21, 25, 28
        Fall of the House of Usher, The 38, 49, 58
        Jeux 52-53
        Le Martyre de Saint Sebastien 50-51
        Pelleas et Melisande 7, 24, 29, 30, 32, 36-38, 43, 49, 50
        Rodrigue et Chimene 24, 26
      orchestral and chamber
        Cello Sonata 57
        Images 7, 46-47
        La Mer 7, 10, 43-45, 46, 53
        Nocturnes 7, 18, 32-33
        Prelude a 'l'Apres-midi d'un faune' 5, 6, 7, 17, 18, 27, 51, 53
        Printemps 18, 19
        String Quartet 26, 32
        Symphony in B minor 14
        Syrinx 53
        Violin Sonata 57-58
      piano works
        Arabesques 21
        En blanc et noir 57
        Children's Corner 47
        "Clair de lune" 21
        Estampes 38-39
        Etudes 57, 60
        Fetes galantes 41
        L'Isle joyeux 41
        Masques 41
        Petit Suite 21
        Pour le piano 34
        Preludes 48-49
        Suite bergamasque 21
      songs
        Beau Soir 22
        Le Lilas 22
        Mandoline 22
        Le Promenoir des deux amants 53
        Proses lyriques 28
        Les Roses 22
        Three Ballads of Francois Villon 53
  as critic 47-48
  death of 60
  illness of 47, 57-58
  influence of 60
  loves of
    Bardac, Emma 39-40, 42-43, 45, 56, 58, 60
    Dupont, Gabrielle 6, 26, 30, 35
    Leblanc, Georgette 36
    Texier, Rosalie "Lily" 32, 35, 39-40, 42
    Vasnier, Madame Marie-Blanche 14-15, 22, 40
  and poetry 5, 7, 17, 24, 27, 28, 34, 50, 52, 53
  prizes and awards of 10, 12, 15, 39
  student days 10-12
  as tutor 13
Debussy Adele (sister) 8
Debussy Claude-Emma "Chouchou" (daughter) 45, 47
Debussy Manuel-Achille (father) 7, 9, 20
Debussy Victorine (mother) 7
Diaghilev, Serge 51-52
Dukas, Paul 21
Dupont, Gabrielle 6-26, 30, 35
Durand, Jaques 21, 43

Exposition Universelle 22-23

Fleurville, Madame Maute de 10, 21

Guiraud, Ernest 12

Hartmann, Georges 30

Impressionism 7, 19

Lavignac, Albert 11
Leblanc, Georgette 36
Liszt, Franz 18

Maeterlinck, Maurice 24, 29, 36, 42
Mallarme, Stephane 5, 7, 27, 28, 52-53
Marmontel, Antoine 11
Meck, Madame Nadezhda von 13, 14
Meck, Sophie von 55
Monet, Claude 19
Moreau-Sainti, Madame 14
Mussorgsky, Modeste 23, 42

Nijinsky, Vaclav 51-52

Poe, Edgar Allan 24, 38
Pre-Raphaelites 16, 21

Ravel, Maurice 28, 32, 52, 60
Renoir, Pierre Auguste 19
Roger, Therese 28
Rossetti, Dante Gabriel 16, 21
Roustan, Clementine 10

Saint-Saens, Camille 5, 56
Satie, Erik 26, 28
Schoenberg, Arnold 24
Stravinsky, Igor 24, 51, 53, 60
Symbolism 7, 24-25

Tchaikovsky, Peter Ilych 13
Texier, Rosalie "Lily" 32, 35, 39-40, 42

Vasnier, Madame Marie-Blanche 14-15, 22, 40
Vasnier, Monsieur 14, 16, 18
Verlaine, Paul 21
Villa Medici 15-18
Villon, Francois 53
Vines, Ricardo 39

Wagner, Richard 11, 16-17, 21, 22, 24, 30
War 9, 56-57
Whistler, James McNeill 16